About Island Press

Since 1984, the nonprofit organization Island Press has been stimulating, shaping, and communicating ideas that are essential for solving environmental problems worldwide. With more than 1,000 titles in print and some 30 new releases each year, we are the nation's leading publisher on environmental issues. We identify innovative thinkers and emerging trends in the environmental field. We work with world-renowned experts and authors to develop cross-disciplinary solutions to environmental challenges.

Island Press designs and executes educational campaigns, in conjunction with our authors, to communicate their critical messages in print, in person, and online using the latest technologies, innovative programs, and the media. Our goal is to reach targeted audiences—scientists, policy makers, environmental advocates, urban planners, the media, and concerned citizens—with information that can be used to create the framework for long-term ecological health and human well-being.

Island Press gratefully acknowledges major support from The Bobolink Foundation, Caldera Foundation, The Curtis and Edith Munson Foundation, The Forrest C. and Frances H. Lattner Foundation, The JPB Foundation, The Kresge Foundation, The Summit Charitable Foundation, Inc., and many other generous organizations and individuals.

The opinions expressed in this book are those of the author(s) and do not necessarily reflect the views of our supporters.

A HEALTHY NATURE Handbook

A HEALTHY NATURE Handbook

Illustrated Insights for
Ecological Restoration
from Volunteer Stewards of
Chicago Wilderness

Edited by

*Justin Pepper
and
Don Parker*

 ISLANDPRESS | Washington | Covelo

 bobolink
FOUNDATION

Writing, editing, design, and illustration by Don Parker Creative, Justin Pepper and Bobolink Foundation, and credited contributors. Cover art by Carrie Carlson Art.

The mission of the Bobolink Foundation is to advance conservation and stewardship of biodiversity through the protection of natural areas, education, and building local constituencies for nature.

bobolinkfoundation.org

Library of Congress Control Number: 2021943899

All Island Press books are printed on environmentally responsible materials.

Manufactured in the United States of America
10 9 8 7 6 5 4 3 2

Keywords: biodiversity, bobolink, Chicago region, community, community building, environment, forest preserve districts, grassland habitat, grassroots movement, habitat, monitor, native seed production, prairie, restoration, sedge, seeding approaches, steward, wetland habitat, wilderness

Table of Contents

For Tom

Your clarity, commitment, wisdom, and generosity will guide us. Your work continues.

Preface

This book started on a walk through Somme Woods in Northbrook, Illinois. We (Don and Justin) were each embarking on a new professional chapter and decided to catch up at one of the special places where we've volunteered over the years to help restore native habitat. The discussion turned to volunteer stewardship.

Where do aspiring stewards go for good information? Who is capturing the tried-and-true insights of top-level restoration practitioners? How are we sharing this vital work with the next generation of leaders and inviting their innovations?

"What we need is a *Cook's Illustrated* for habitat restoration," one of us said. The magazine's well-tested recipes, equipment reviews, and discussion of techniques and ingredients help home chefs raise their game. While professionals may also gain plenty, *Cooks's* aim is distinctly DIY. So was ours.

And so we started contacting practitioners we knew who had notably advanced some aspect of habitat restoration, particularly individuals who have surfaced perennially for us as reliable sources of insight. After sitting with them, we attempted to channel their wisdom and recreate the experience of being shoulder-to-shoulder with them in the field, knowing a book is only a starting point. This effort owes everything to their generosity of time and expertise.

Those featured in this book aren't the only ones with valuable knowledge to share. The contributions of other volunteer leaders could fill several more volumes, to say nothing of our region's professional restorationists. We've attempted to open a window into this world; yet, with only six chapters, this is far from a complete picture of our region's ecosystem of conservationists.

As we've created this book, society has gone through more than a few moments of reckoning, particularly around issues of equity. Restoration is a social endeavor, and we have long recognized that the participants do not adequately reflect the social diversity of our region. The events of recent years underscore not only the pressing need to change this, but also the opportunity.

In response to COVID-19, we saw unprecedented visitation to natural areas as people from all neighborhoods, and in record numbers, sought peace, connection, beauty, and sunshine. In the Chicago region, nature is not a luxury for the few but a right of residency, thanks to the vision of the civic leaders who created the forest preserves more than a century ago. As we strive for a more equitable region in the months and years ahead, let us seek common purpose and new collaborations to better deliver the benefits of this legacy to all our neighbors, whether in the form of natural climate solutions, increased physical and emotional well-being, or happier, more nature-rich childhoods. This tumultuous year has proven we all need nature. Let's act with the knowledge that nature needs all of us, too.

Though not always explicitly called out, the backdrop for most of the following chapters is the committed staff of the region's landowning agencies working alongside empowered volunteer leaders. Those agencies perform near heroics on shoestring budgets and play important roles in supporting and facilitating volunteers. None of them are sufficiently funded to address all the needs of the lands they hold for us, and this should change. But even if it does, volunteer stewardship will remain an indispensable tool for providing the level of site-specific, long-term commitment fundamental to sustaining the land's health.

A note about science: this is not a peer-reviewed journal. It has been thoroughly practitioner-reviewed, however. While some of the field work presented here is early and experimental, much of it has been refined over decades, resulting in some of the best restorations anywhere. These are successful, local examples; they worked for these stewards in these microclimates, at this time, on these sites. Your results may be different. We welcome other practitioners, as well as researchers, to investigate assertions and deepen our collective understanding of how habitat restoration is most effectively accomplished. Continual improvement is critical to the growth of restoration as a field.

The urgent need for efforts like this one was driven home in devastating fashion as we developed this project. Our initial intention was to feature Tom Vanderpoel in more chapters, given his logical, sequential approach to successful restorations. We were in final edits on *Reclaiming Sedge Meadow*, our prototype chapter, when Tom suddenly passed away. When we lost Tom, we lost not only a remarkable, kind, and inspirational human being, but also a wellspring of hard-earned ecological wisdom.

Tom's time on the planet was too short. That's true for all of us working to preserve and restore biodiversity. The still-young pursuit of ecological restoration continues to evolve. As we develop better techniques and clearer understandings of these deeply complex systems, we nourish something magical and beyond our individual selves – a living culture whose vibrancy is reflected in the land.

Introduction

Not so long ago, I hosted a new conservation friend – a skilled field botanist – who was launching an ambitious multi-state grassland conservation effort in the southeastern U.S. My plan was to take him on a tour of several prairie restorations of various ages around the Chicago region, to show results and talk about how we approach the work here in the Home of Volunteer Stewardship.

As still too few realize, over the course of the last four decades, people here have learned what it takes to keep nature healthy through hands-on effort and observation. This culture of conservation and the revival of natural communities across thousands of acres of protected land has largely been accomplished on weekends and evenings by pipefitters, pharmacists, teachers, marketing professionals, accountants, and artists. That is to say, normal people.

Well, kind of normal people. In the same way anyone who steps forward to solve a problem that means something to them and their community is "normal." Along the way, many of these everyday folks have become leading experts in species and natural systems, innovators in the field (literally). Unbound by convention, they create new ways to heal nature.

This day, I was going to share some of their outstanding results with my visitor. Coming down off a dry gravel hill prairie remnant, we entered the first and youngest restoration we would visit. Hiding under the midsummer grasses, the botanist quickly spied a single stalk of prairie skullcap, *Scutellaria leonardii*.

"You've got *Scutellaria*? No one has *Scutellaria*!" He was right. This was going to be a fun day.

Later, pausing in a more established restoration, my new friend shook his head in disbelief. "I spend a lot of time in remnant natural areas looking for rare plants," he said. "If someone dropped me here, I would assume this was a remnant. It looks better than most I see. This is blowing my mind; I just didn't know this was even possible."

That was my exact reaction when I learned that we can restore ecosystems. It expanded my notion of what is possible, and it is why I moved to the Chicago area originally. Upon arriving, I dedicated weekends to time in the field working with and learning from more experienced restoration practitioners. It remains one of my favorite things to do. What a privilege it is to work and walk with someone who can help you repair a precious piece of our planet. We should all know the gratification that comes from committing to nurturing a place, the pride of healing.

More recently, I've had the chance to travel widely, seeing some of the best conservation happening throughout the hemisphere. Against this broader perspective, the community of ordinary-extraordinary people that originally drew me here only looks more impressive. Their work, their individual and collective example, has grown only more relevant – especially now, as budgets tighten and our species grows increasingly urban. They show how we can have healthy nature at the heart of a thriving metropolis, and how satisfying it can be to get your hands dirty for a cause that you care about.

The work is complicated, but not unknowable. If you learn which details matter, focus on them, and do the right things in the right places at the right times. It works.

So how does one learn which details are critical and which are distractions?

The best way is in the field, alongside a successful practitioner. No publication can replace that, and that is not our aim.

Preserving and sharing the wealth of hard-earned knowledge across our region will require deliberate efforts to capture – for practical use and for posterity – the processes, techniques, philosophies, and everyday details of restoration. This is just one such effort. We do this not as a final word on any subject, but to mark a point in our field's evolution.

Beyond just sharing repeatable recipes, we hope to expose the thinking behind successful restorations to a wider audience. For current stewards, we hope you find value in this effort that you can apply in the field. The practice of restoration evolves and improves through the sharing of experiences. We hope you will not only read this, but also contribute your own successes, techniques, questions, and challenges. What we have learned together over the years is a kind of real-life magic that needs to be shared widely.

For anyone new or not yet involved, we have a slightly different aim – an invitation, really. We want you to know that restoring health to ecosystems is possible, and that restoration has been practiced and propelled forward in no small part by the commitment and creativity of nonprofessionals. Chicago is rich with protected nature, and there is no larger community of grassroots conservationists anywhere. These generous, fun people head out into nearby nature each and every weekend. They would love to meet you. Our natural areas would, too.

Justin Pepper
Bobolink Foundation
August 2021

Acknowledgments

This guide has come together through the generosity of many people who have given their time, knowledge, and sweat to create this tool for the conservation community. We'd like to thank the following:

Throughout the Guide

To all who work to preserve and care for natural land, and especially every volunteer who has come to a workday or given something of themselves to better connect us to nature. Carrie Suzanne Carlson, for her soulful art celebrating this region's ecological riches. Bobby Sutton, for his evocative time-lapse restoration sequences at the heart of this effort, and for his culture-building illustrations in general. Stephen Packard, for his guidance and mentorship over many years, including for this guide. Karen Glennemeier for science and numbers advice. The Prairie Enthusiasts, for the Parsnip Predator. Clifford Schultz for his twisted brushpile technique. Daniel Suarez for general stewardship and leadership insights. Jim Vanderpoel, Bernie Buchholz, Daniel Suarez, Cody Considine, John McCabe, Jim Root, Benjamin Cox, Ed Collins, Becky Collings, Kevin Scheiwiller, Donna Bolzman, Ken Klick, Peter Whitney, Stephen Smith, Eriko Kojima, Kathy Garness, and Laurel Ross for reviewing parts or all of this guide and helping improve it. Catherine Game at Brushwood Center at Ryerson Woods for pointing us toward some wonderful artists. Gary Glowacki of Lake County Forest Preserves and Allison Sacerdote-Velat at the Peggy Notebaert Nature Museum for deeply informing our thinking around wildlife management and monitoring.

Restoration, Nachusa Style

Jay Stacy, Bernie Buchholz, Cody Considine, Bill Kleiman, and Kaleb Baker for sitting down with us, giving us a tour of Nachusa, and for providing a considerable amount of folllow-up information. Philip Juras, for his incredible ability to capture native ecosystems with his brush. John Vanek for sharing his Nachusa plantings map. Also David Crites and Damian Considine for contributing to our conversation around the lunch table in November 2018.

Backyard Seed Factory

Rob Sulski, for his enterprise and openness in sharing his expertise. Stephen Packard and Lake County Forest Preserves ecologist Kelly Schultz at the Lake County Native Plant Nursery for comments on seed propagation and outplanting. Tom Vanderpoel and Stephen Packard for sharing their Sought-After 60 List.

Reclaiming Sedge Meadow

Tom Vanderpoel, Donna Bolzman, Kevin Scheiwiller, and all of the Citizens for Conservation leadership and volunteers. It was their work that inspired much of this project. Kathy Garness, for her fine and studious botanical illustrations. Michael Huft and Carol Freeman for botanical reference. Linda Curtis, for her graceful sedge photos and field expertise.

Monitoring Fit for a Steward

Karen Glennemeier, for sharing her experience working with volunteer monitors across Chicago Wilderness, and patience with our many follow-up questions. Forest Preserves of Cook County Senior Resource Ecologist Rebecca Collings for her valuable feedback around monitoring protocols. Margaret Frisbie, Mark Hauser, and Friends of the Chicago River for sharing the rapid monitoring protocol they use.

Monitor Birds, See Ecosystems in 3D

Jenny Flexman, for sharing insight from decades of volunteer stewardship (as well as delicious squash soup made from her garden), and for taking us out to Schaumburg Road Grasslands to see the breeding birds and to plant plugs. Chris Parson and Jackie Majdov, for giving us a window into aquatic monitoring. Jenny Vogt, for capturing the exuberance of a singing dickcissel. Chip O'Leary and Dennis Nyberg, for their Treelines study that kicked off so much. Karen Glennemeier, for her good numbers advice. Poplar Creek Prairie Stewards, for their decades of dedication. Audubon Great Lakes, Illinois Audubon, and McHenry County Conservation District for their insights into grassland bird habitat preferences. Gordon Hempton, for using his ears and encouraging us to do the same.

The Society of Stewardship

Stephen Packard, Linda Masters, and Eriko Kojima, for their wise and wide-ranging conversations about restoration culture, so much more of which we wished we could fit into this format. Josh Coles, for contributing to our conversation from his experience with the Forest Preserves of Cook County's Centennial Volunteers. Bobby Garro Sutton, for his painting evoking a happy winter workday gone by. Heeyoung Kim, for her exquisite watercolors inspired by her personal discovery of the Somme Preserves in Northbrook.

Restoration, Nachusa Style

with Jay Stacy, Bernie Buchholz,
Cody Considine, Bill Kleiman,
and Kaleb Baker

In 34 years, The Nature Conservancy has transformed Nachusa Grasslands's 4,000 acres, reintroduced bison, and influenced countless other restorations. At the center of the work are volunteers paying fine-grained attention to the land.

Nachusa Grasslands has attracted a lot of press recently – reintroducing bison within a few hours of Chicago will do that. Without a doubt, the cloven celebrities' arrival has been exciting, unleashing a primal force upon the land many believe could be essential to rejuvenate it fully.

Yet the bison are just the latest validation of another primal force, the volunteer-fueled restoration championed by The Nature Conservancy (TNC) since 1986, which has restored a matrix large and robust enough to support this experiment.

The Conservancy first acquired 397 acres of natural remnants – mainly unplowed prairie knobs with sandstone outcrops – in 1986, in the area around Franklin Grove, Illinois. Already in a race with housing developments that have now begun to appear in earnest, TNC continued to acquire some adjoining agricultural fields. It quickly set about

transforming the land back into a patchwork of prairie and savanna with plant community compositions indistinguishable from high-quality remnants.

From the beginning, the restoration has been accomplished by staff and volunteers working side-by-side. This symbiosis has allowed the community to conduct restoration at an ambitious scale while paying close attention to the land's innumerable details.

Born of the volunteer stewardship culture of Chicago, a can-do ethos has evolved on this expanding island of habitat diversity. Stewards and staff have honed restoration techniques based on trial and error, science, and the drive to find new and better ways of doing things.

What has been accomplished at Nachusa is largely the result of a decision Bill Kleiman, Nachusa's longtime preserve manager, made

Doug's Knob, Nachusa Grasslands.

decades ago: that engaging volunteer leaders as equal partners would be at the project's heart. That commitment has paid rich dividends. Some 25 highly dedicated stewards have put in hundreds of thousands of hours over the decades, making key decisions about their sites and building the culture. By Bill's estimate, roughly half of Nachusa's management units now have a volunteer steward. Abetted over the years by thousands of rank-and-file weekend volunteers, their high-quality plantings and carefully tended remnants are the basis (and seed source) from which many new restorations spring.

As the principle architect of Nachusa's conservation culture, Bill had something to do with this success. In fact, we could have written a chapter on him alone – the guy can fix tractors, identify rare sedges, deliver keynotes, orchestrate burns, and restore century-old barns. But we decided not to—and not just because Bill would hate it, but because we feared doing so might make this all too easily

dismissible. Bill is a remarkable person, but what he's done is totally replicable.

How it gets repeated will vary from place to place and person to person. Bill, for one, decided that silent, omnipresent reminders might be helpful. So, label gun in hand, he set out to reinforce the effective use of equipment and organization of shared space. His handiwork encourages, even as it has earned him the moniker "mad labeler." As a nod to Bill, you will find his labels scattered throughout this chapter. We hope they invite reflection on how each of us can support others' commitment wherever we're involved. Ultimately, that's the only way restoration succeeds.

Sewing a Quilt, One Parcel At a Time

Volunteers have played a critical role in stitching a vast native landscape back together, one planting at a time.

Of the 132 plantings at Nachusa to date, volunteer stewards have done 44. Compared with those of the staff crews, their plantings are small, totaling 225 total restored acres as of June 2020. (Adding remnants, volunteers manage about 900 acres.) But they're among Nachusa's best, often buffering and tying together remnants. In some cases, they build on crew plantings. In others, they provide the cornerstone and seed source for more.

❶ 1987–1994
A small crew of staff and volunteers do the first plantings around the original remnant prairie knobs. Bill Kleiman becomes preserve manager in 1993.

❷ 1997–2002
Jay Stacy conducts the first volunteer-led planting at Nachusa, followed by others, converting 31 acres of ag field.

❸ 1999
Hank and Becky Hartman begin restoring 51-acre Big Woods. As they revive savanna and prairie, some call them the "overseeding gods."

❹ 2002–2007
Former Big 10 basketball star Tom Mitchell, working four-day weeks for the IRS, spends two of his other three days planting and caring for four units of Thelma Carpenter Prairie. They remain important seed warrens, especially for coreopsis.

❺ 2004–2007
A young father and innovative botanist, Chris Hauser burns the candle at both ends to plant 13 acres at Clear Creek South.

❻ 2006–2013
Al and Mary Meier's five plantings connect remnant dry prairies at Dot and Doug Wade Prairie, including a redo of a failed 1994 crew planting. The couple gets up each morning at 4:00 am to drive from Bloomington-Normal.

❼ 2006–2015
In 10 separate plantings, Bernie Buchholz, with wife Cindy, plants 48 acres of dry mesic prairie surrounding a remnant knob. They spend much time restoring the remnant itself.

❽ 2006–2010
Jay plants five sites up north in tandem with the Buchholzes, forming a block. In 2012, he plants 16 acres of prairie to the west, which he claims are his last.

9 2008 & 2012
High-school biology teacher Mary Vieregg, with husband Jim, plants 10 acres of prairie nearby at Dropseed Hills North.

10 1995–2018
As TNC refines techniques and adds equipment, crew plantings increase in size, including a giant 103-acre effort in 2016.

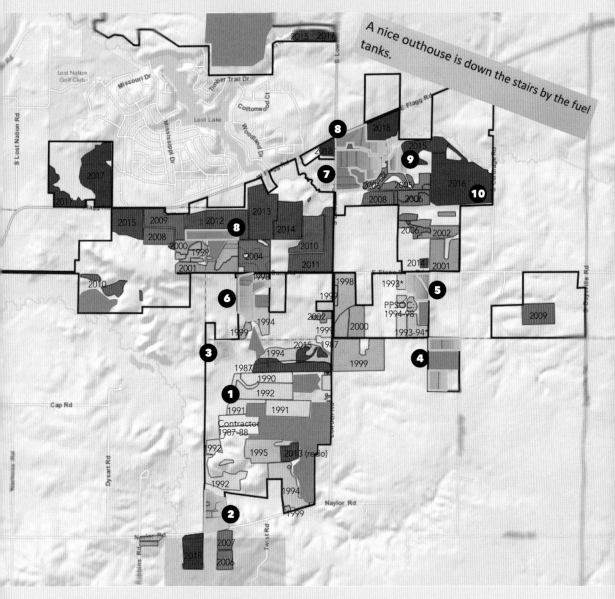

Year labels = staff plantings (or *previous owner). Turquoise = volunteer plantings. Pale yellow to dark red = older planting to more recent. Remnants = green. Smaller plantings omitted.

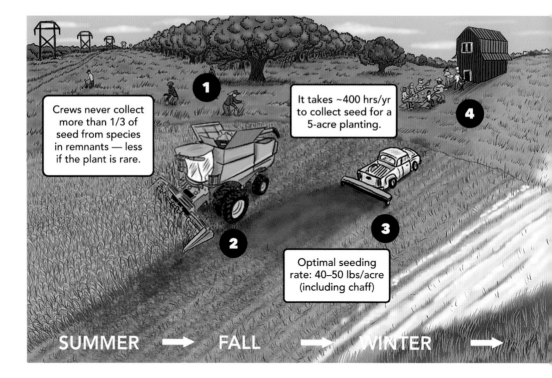

Crews never collect more than 1/3 of seed from species in remnants — less if the plant is rare.

It takes ~400 hrs/yr to collect seed for a 5-acre planting.

Optimal seeding rate: 40–50 lbs/acre (including chaff)

SUMMER ➡ FALL ➡ WINTER ➡

Restoration at Scale

At Nachusa, each new land acquisition is a chance to expand native habitat. Here's their formula for turning farm fields back to prairie.

❶ Find Remnants
Even just a few conservative plants can signify a remnant ecosystem. Defend them. Remnants are your best seed source until your plantings expand. Scout often, weed, and connect them with other remnants.

❷ Clean the Slate
Avoid seeding into weedy areas. Most Nachusa plantings begin as ag fields, where years of weed control with glyphosate depletes the invasive seed bank. Before planting, harvest the corn or soy, leaving stubble to prevent erosion.

❸ Plant Seed
Use a diverse mix collected from onsite remnants (and increasingly, plantings) if possible. Get seed out by Thanksgiving – not-yet-frozen soils will hold seed in place. Freezing and thawing will integrate seeds into soil and break seed coats.

❹ Be Social
Nachusa's stewardship community bonds over informal gatherings: lunch breaks in the HQ barn, dinner at Bill's, a drink on the porch after the work is done. This is as essential to success as seeding or tractor maintenance.

It takes ~17 hrs/acre/yr to weed a new planting.

April–May:
90% weeds
10% seeds

Sep–Nov:
10% weeds
90% seeds

SPRING ➡ SUMMER ➡ FALL ➡ WINTER

❺ Weed (And Collect Seed)

Start weeding as soon as you can ID spring seedlings. (Sweet clover and birdsfoot trefoil are prime targets at Nachusa.) Weeding is the main focus this time of year in new plantings. By year three, though, make time to collect seed from early bloomers such as violets. Sow them immediately if you CAN.

❻ Collect Seed

Nachusa stewards spend increasingly more time collecting seed from established plantings as the growing season progresses. In first-year plantings, the plants are very small, with a few annuals and quick perennials blooming. But the list of blooming plants grows each year. In some areas, such as Nachusa's one-acre dropseed garden, stewards and crew now even collect seed with a combine.

❼ Overseed

Fill gaps and increase species count. Target areas that may support missing plant associates. (See "Focus Your Overseeding," page 17.)

❽ Burn

Prescribed burns are essential to remnants and restorations. Burn a new planting as early as year one. Mow the dried stalks of still-sparse new plantings to make it easier to find weeds in year two and to concentrate fuel enough to carry fire. (Mow as late into fall as possible to leave wildlife habitat, but, ideally, before the ground freezes.) Nachusa burns are varied. Even among prairies, some burn yearly, some every other year, and some every third year. Woodlands have their own regimes.

Growing an Effective Volunteer Culture

Tips for nurturing a thriving stewardship community.

Ditch your volunteer program.
The first rule of Nachusa's volunteer program: there is no volunteer program. "It's a culture; it's a community," says Cody. There's no hierarchy, not even a volunteer coordinator. Stewards are 100 percent peers and colleagues, says Bill.

Lead by example.
"I would get here 8:30, 8:15, and Bill's been out to work for an hour already. He's been going around on a tractor, mowing stuff," says Jay. "There's nobody sittin' around. And that inspires a volunteer, because we want our time to matter."

Empower, don't control.
"I've been asked by people from other projects, how do you control the volunteers?" says Bernie. "And the answer is, of course, we don't control." Stewards move toward the landowner's vision from their own angles. "It was Bill's genius as a manager that he would empower appropriate people and find the best way they could serve this project," says Jay. "Your run-of-the-mill managers tend to want to keep all the reins in their hands. And Bill's the opposite. He would say, 'Go out and do it.'"

New freshener. Like it or not?

Do real work.

As Jay puts it, volunteers aren't just for "dinky stuff."
"People get into the heart of the work the first day,"
he says. "Volunteers collect seed, manage weeds,
make up most of our fire crew," says Bill. "They
run our festival, tours program, education program, website,
butterfly monitoring, bird monitoring, some of our rare species work.
Two volunteers pick up roadside trash and others help care for the headquarters.
Another does carpentry tasks, and so on." Stewards regularly plan and implement entire
projects, says Bill. "I try to say yes to big ideas."

Let Dee know.

Hand stewards ownership (and keys).

"Stewards love to have a piece of the preserve they can call their own," says Bill. "They get to know
it well." Hand them the keys to the headquarters, gates, and tools, too. "Our stewards are out seven
days a week, early in the mornings, sometimes late at night," he says. Bill and Cody estimate that at
least 60 percent of volunteer restoration work takes place outside official workdays.

Make time for community.

Being around Nachusa people, you get the impression they must always be laughing. "At the end
of the day, you tie it all together with something besides work," says steward Dave Crites. "And
something that everyone can relax and relate to, and have conversations about what they do outside
of here. There is a potluck or a cookout or something pretty much every month." Find ways to
express genuine appreciation, too.

Always keep the door open.

"On the fourth day of a heat wave, somebody comes in here and starts asking these kind of entry-level
questions – 'What are you doing? How many bison?'" says Bernie. "Bill engages people that don't
have any apparent immediate payoff." You've got to stay open, says Jay. "The person that's gonna be
your best volunteer, odds-on, is going to come at the moment when you least want them to."

Beloved Dish Washers:
- Use soap and warm water.
- Wash both sides of drinking glasses, plates

The Humming
Lunch Table

Never mind modern burn gear, giant combines, or mapping software – a half-dozen folding lunch tables constitute one of the technologies key to Nachusa's success.

A renovated two-story barn serves as The Nature Conservancy office, supply depot, seed processing area, and garage. On the second floor, a large multi-purpose area with a wraparound view of the rolling savanna is part conference room, part break room, part office, part library. But every midday, it's the lunch room.

"There is a conversation that happens at lunch," says Bernie, "about a species, about what worked on this weed, how I'm getting this to grow, so that there is a continually developing conversation about what works, and how do I make my planting the best it can be – call it 'best practices.' We just want it to be better and better and better."

The most common lunchtime topic? "What seed is ready where," says Jay. "What are you getting, everybody? You know, there's a patch there I didn't touch – go get that." Crews recently began mapping seed with ArcGIS. Yet the lunch table, like a beehive with scouts reporting in on nectar locations, still provides a vital link to understanding the landscape at any given moment.

"I think the *lingua franca* out here is knowledge," says Bernie. "The exchange is knowledge. And I'd rather know; I'd rather be able to tell Jay about an experience with a species than almost anything. We want to know, and we want to share."

It's part of the ongoing learning culture, from beginners to veterans. "We learn by trial and error," says Jay. "There's not one of us who hasn't had too much of a species. And people come in at lunch going, 'Oh shoot, you know, we put in this, and I put in too much of this and this.'" Increasingly, scientists sit around the table, too. "We might have 25 research projects underway," says Bernie. "Sometimes there might be 15 scientists, or their helpers, sitting at this table at lunch. That's a lot of energy, and I think it's a huge opportunity."

"There are certain physical things that can really help support conservation work," says Cody, "and one is this barn. A central meeting place, a place to meet someone at lunchtime. You may be all over heck during the day, but lunch is the time you come back and share ideas. Places like this are critical if you want to foster a very community-oriented management of the land."

How To
Hold and Expand a Planting

Expanding a restoration across thousands of acres is a bit like defending a sprawling ancient empire from marauders. Here's how they do it at Nachusa.

1. **Battle weeds with seeds.** Establish your planting so well that it's virtually impregnable. The more densely and diversely you plant, the more resistant to invasives (and the better seed source later). Weed infiltrators like crazy. "You win the battle or lose it in the first two years," says Jay.

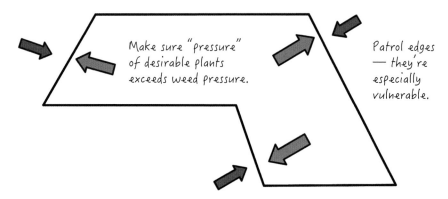

Make sure "pressure" of desirable plants exceeds weed pressure.

Patrol edges — they're especially vulnerable.

2. **Protection through expansion.** When your original planting is solid — with no internal infestations — you can add territory. Minimize edges by creating a solid shape. (This also makes it easier to burn.) Avoid planting isolated outposts or skinny corridors, as they're easily overtaken.

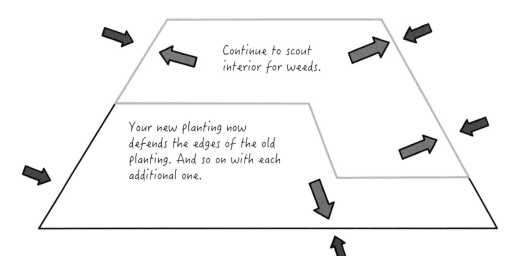

Continue to scout interior for weeds.

Your new planting now defends the edges of the old planting. And so on with each additional one.

How to Defend Edges?

Nachusa Plants a Common-Species Border

If your planting adjoins a weedy area, try seeding a 6- to 10-foot border of common native species. Depending on habitat, this could include hoary vervain, wild bergamot, black-eyed Susans, yellow coneflower, and lots of Canada rye — all seed that's easy to get. These fast-growing species can hold off some invaders. If you do see infestations, you can spot treat with broadleaf herbicide and worry less about off-target casualties. Your hardy natives will fill in any gaps you create. When you're ready (such as after you've planted the adjacent area), you can overseed with a richer mix.

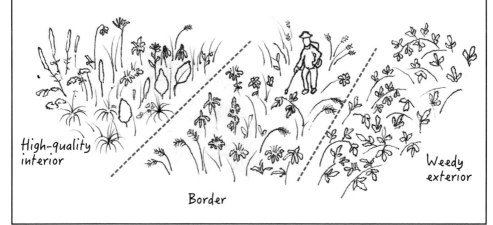

High-quality interior

Border

Weedy exterior

Herbicide-Tolerant Plantings

To more efficiently establish stable new plantings, Cody Considine is experimenting with what he calls Herbicide Resistant Prairie Restoration. It starts with a fall seeding of known Transline-resistant species. (Seventy-two have been identified so far, including *Castilleja sessiliflora*, *Dalea purpurea*, and *Zizia aptera*.) After letting the seedlings get established for one growing season, he boom-sprays with Transline until the invasive seedbank is exhausted—one to two growing seasons. Then he overseeds with the rest of the species that don't tolerate Transline. While this approach relies heavily on herbicide, the spraying period is finite. Based on what he's seen so far, Cody believes this practice will have its place in large-scale restorations.

SAFETY GLASSES?

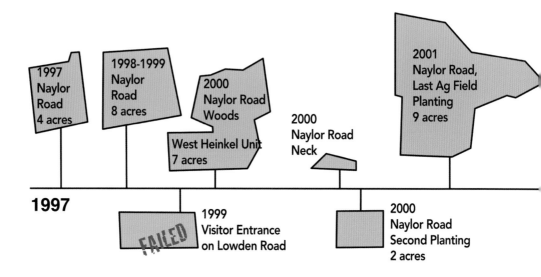

1997

1997
Naylor
Road
4 acres

1998-1999
Naylor
Road
8 acres

2000
Naylor Road
Woods

West Heinkel Unit
7 acres

2000
Naylor Road
Neck

2001
Naylor Road,
Last Ag Field
Planting
9 acres

FAILED

1999
Visitor Entrance
on Lowden Road

2000
Naylor Road
Second Planting
2 acres

Jay's Portfolio

A steward breaks down how he spends his time.

As one of the longest-running volunteer stewards at Nachusa, Jay Stacy has devoted the past 26 years of his life to transforming 85 acres of cornfield into beautiful native prairie — 12 separate plantings in total. (He also stewards 65 acres of remnants and restorations.) A look at his "portfolio" shows the changing nature of sites' demands.

Early Plantings

Jay's first planting was in 1997. With all his plantings ahead of him, he spent most of his time collecting seed. Today, in 2021, his early restorations require little maintenance: "We've long ago won the weed battle," Jay says. "I go in there a couple times a year, sweet clover time." He also patrols the edges and weeds the roadside every spring. "But I don't add any seeds. I mean, I've added everything from soup to nuts. The things that were appropriate came up and increased, the things that started and were less appropriate came up for a few years and died out, and now it's on its own. There is an endpoint. Otherwise, who could do it? We know the sweet smell of success."

Jay's Time in 1997*

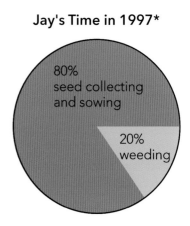

80%
seed collecting
and sowing

20%
weeding

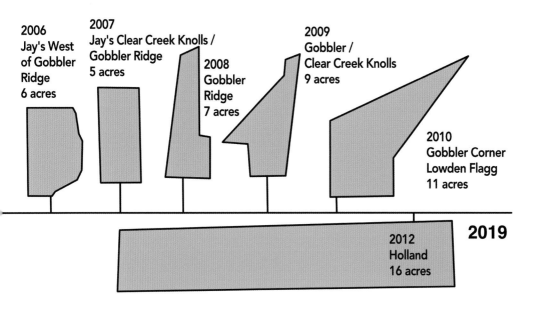

2006
Jay's West of Gobbler Ridge
6 acres

2007
Jay's Clear Creek Knolls / Gobbler Ridge
5 acres

2008
Gobbler Ridge
7 acres

2009
Gobbler / Clear Creek Knolls
9 acres

2010
Gobbler Corner Lowden Flagg
11 acres

2012
Holland
16 acres

2019

Middle Plantings

Back when Jay was planting these re-creations (spending up to 60 hours a week), he'd spend half his time weeding earlier plantings and half collecting seed for the next one. Now, he says, these have all the seed they need. "Weed-wise, the middle plantings are on a scale between Naylor and the Holland 16 acres. The earlier they are, the less I have to check them. Like the '06 in Gobbler, I check that three times a year. The '09 and '10 still have sweet and red clover issues, but way reduced from what it was."

Jay's Time in 2008*

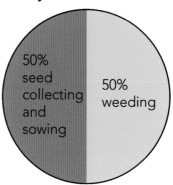

50% seed collecting and sowing

50% weeding

New Plantings

Though Jay's last planting was eight years ago, it still demands most of his time — about 35 hours a week in the growing season. "Every bad thing that can happen has happened," he says, citing floods that eroded a hillside in 2013 and brought in many weeds. "I spend 80% of my weed time in the 16," he says. "The rest of my plantings are all on the way to becoming native carpets, and this one is gonna be no different if I have anything to say about it."

Jay's Time in 2019*

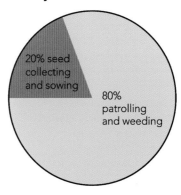

20% seed collecting and sowing

80% patrolling and weeding

Burning, a core part of management, is done collectively by staff and volunteers and not included here. Jay served on the burn crew for 17 years.

Seeding the Grassland

Whether they're being collected, sown, stored, or shared, seeds drive most everything at Nachusa. Some insights from stewards and staff.

Collect All Growing Season

Many groups collect seed in fall. The most successful restorations include spring flora too. Begin collecting when spring ephemerals are ready — as soon as late April for plants such as Whitlow grass and pussytoes.

Plant in Fall, Not Spring

Except for some early-seeding species, sow seed in fall, just before Thanksgiving. That gives seeds a full winter of freezing and thawing, soaking and drying, to break down the seed coat and work into the soil.

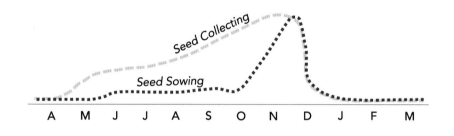

Seed Collecting

Seed Sowing

A   M   J   J   A   S   O   N   D   J   F   M

Set Up Seed Routes like a FedEx Driver

When seed is ready, success is all about hustle. "I'll go out here, and on the way, I'll get this here and here," says Jay. "And you just cover that whole route, *boom, boom, boom* — all of a sudden, in a morning. You can't screw around."

Chaff Is Okay

When collecting, don't worry if stems end up in your bag or bucket. By being as hands-off as possible and cutting seedheads straight into your bag, you can move faster — and save your fingers.

Don't waste time cleaning seed. Nachusa stewards just throw it into their hammer mill to be roughly processed into the mix. The chaff actually helps space seed out when sowing.

Year 1 = Year 100

As much as possible, plant in year one every species you want in year 100. Don't leave out the conservatives for later.

Focus Your Overseeding

That said, augmentation is always possible. "You can tell when a species really likes a spot," says Jay. "They're bigger, and there are more of them — it's just a look they give. Then you look it up in Swink and Wilhelm. What are the associates? You get a 20-species list, and just go seed in that area. We call that *focused overseeding*.

"So you try and build plant communities. You go to a natural area; especially if the soils aren't homogenous, you're gonna come on one community, then a different one. We're trying to imitate that."

EXPERIMENT CORNER

How Much Seed Is Enough?

What's the optimal amount of seed to use when planting? How do you get maximum plant density and diversity without wasting seed?

Bill wanted to put those questions to science. So in 2006, he teamed up with researchers David Goldblum, Brian Glaves, and Lesley Rigg, seeding 72 plots with a dry prairie seed mix, leaving 18 unseeded plots as controls. Sowing at 10, 30, 50, and 70 lbs/acre, they found that after two years, plots with more seed showed considerably greater diversity, conservatism, native plant density, and resistance to weeds. The difference between 50 and 70 lbs/acre, though, was far less significant.

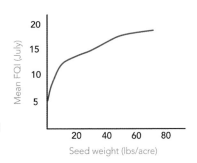

Bill's takeaway: for new plantings, use 40 to 50 pounds of seed per acre (with chaff).*

*As every site is different, adapt your approach as needed. Research published in the June 2013 issue of *Ecological Restoration*.

Do Something Beautifully

What do you do when you're staring at thousands of acres, weeds encroaching, and not enough seed to plant it all?

"Take two acres and do something beautifully," says Jay.

Bernie agrees. "I believe in higher-quality, smaller plantings," he says. "We call these boutique plantings because they're so finely executed. Everybody's trying to do the most beautiful plot — and they are lovely!"

Is it a luxury to invest so much time into so few acres? "We may be entering a time now where volume is gonna be more important," says Jay. "If we want to expand and buy more land, we may have to demonstrate that we can keep pace. The crew has been doing 100 acres a year. That's a tremendous amount to do a high-quality planting. It's a testament to them."

The two approaches may not be mutually exclusive. Experience suggests that volunteers' investment in small, boutique plantings can pay big dividends.

The visual impact of a painstakingly tended area is an ad for restoration, says Jay. "Your employees and your volunteers can come and celebrate and be inspired. Your visitors can come and see what can be done."

A high-quality restoration also can drive fundraising. "We realized pretty soon when we saw the response to them that we were doing these as exemplars for donors," says Bernie.

Small, boutique plantings have practical, functional benefits, too, and can serve as a cornerstone for larger plantings. "If that two acres is nice," says Kaleb, "you're not doing weed management there, meaning you have more time to spend on weeds in the other 98 acres, let's say. You also can more easily collect seed for planting more acres the next year; so then that 98 becomes 95. And over time, you exponentially reduce your workload. Each year you do a planting, you have a new seed resource."

Nachusa staff buy time and keep weeds and brush out of new acquisitions by keeping the land in corn or soy until they're ready for planting.

Even if the boutique approach is a luxury, it's one that volunteers, giving of their own time and passion for the land, make possible. It takes the calculation from a strict cost-benefit analysis into the realm of joy and purpose.

"Jay was talking about these small plantings being for donors and such," says Bernie. "But it's also for me. It's what's satisfying for me."

Notes

About Jay Stacy

In 1996, Jay was selling clothes in a high-end Michigan Avenue shop. An avid birder, he drove out to Nachusa one day, on a tip about grasshopper sparrows and upland plovers. He saw both birds within five minutes, and stayed to become one of Nachusa's longest-serving volunteer stewards.

About Bernie Buchholz

Long a "50-dollar-member" of TNC, Bernie went to a workday and never stopped coming. In Nachusa, he found "the perfect antidote to a 20-year career in finance." He's been a steward since 2006 and was a leading founder of Friends of Nachusa Grasslands. The nonprofit (nachusagrasslands.org) has given $210,000 in research grants and raised $2 million for endowments to care for the grasslands in perpetuity.

About Cody Considine

Growing up in nearby Dixon, Cody first joined the Nachusa crew in 2005 as a technician. For his graduate thesis, he studied fire history at TNC's Kankakee Sands Preserve. Now deputy director, he supports all restoration and management operations, including overseeing burns, hiring crews, and leading the bison program.

About Bill Kleiman

Nachusa's first and only full-time preserve manager, Bill has built the program into a flagship example of large-scale habitat restoration. A founder of the Illinois Prescribed Fire Council and leader of the Grassland Restoration Network, he has mentored generations of conservationists.

About Kaleb Baker

Kaleb started as a Saturday volunteer, later joining the crew as a technician for two seasons and pursuing his MS in ecology, including a thesis on honeysuckle control. He chaired the stewardship committee for the Franklin Creek Conservation Association.

About The Nature Conservancy

One of the world's leading conservation organizations, The Nature Conservancy has roots in nearby Rockford. As owner of Nachusa Grasslands, it has long empowered the project with staff, training, funds, and land acquisition, as well as support for its innovative approach to restoration.

The Parsnip Predator
WITH THE PRAIRIE ENTHUSIASTS

The phototoxic wild parsnip, *Pastinaca sativa*, can give those who touch it (especially its sap) a burning rash and skin discoloration. To remove this pernicious invasive while minimizing contact with it, The Prairie Enthusiasts, a Wisconsin-based group, cleverly modified a light shovel to create the Parsnip Predator. The group produces them for sale on their website, theprairieenthusiasts.org. Other weed spades, including the Root Slayer, are also available commercially.

The handle is turned 90° to make cutting easier.

Push the blade into the soil at an angle, cutting the root several inches beneath the surface. Slice straight, as prying can bend or break the blade (although newer models are stronger). Bag the cut parsnip, but handle carefully. Wear gloves, pants, and long sleeves.

cut

Cut the plant after it has sent up its flowering stem but before seed set, usually mid-July.

The blade has been narrowed and sharpened, with a notch for centering on the root.

The predator is also good for other tap-rooted weeds such as sweet clover.

Backyard
Seed Factory

with Rob Sulski

Propagating the high-quality, diminutive species that too often get left out of restorations.

In a competition of floristic quality, Rob Sulski's yard would beat yours. And mine. Even most natural areas. Everywhere you look, uncommon native violets, phloxes, and puccoons abound, surrounded by clouds of happy pollinators. Since 2005, Rob has been propagating plants as a volunteer at his suburban Glenview home, supplying high volumes of conservative seed and plugs to local habitat restorations. His quarter-acre property produces gallons of seed, and between 4,000 and 6,000 plant plugs a year. At any given time, he's working on more than 50 species.

The work started as a short-order planting and rescue. In 2006, the Village of Northbrook was constructing a flood-detention basin next to the Glenbrook North Prairie Nature Preserve, where Rob was a volunteer steward. The village's plan required revegetating a buffer area around the prairie with natives. "At that point I said, 'Well, the quickest way to do that is to start growing some of these things.'" Through propagation, Rob also saved many mesic upland species that were threatened by the temporarily altered hydrology.

"So I started growing, growing, and then people said, 'Whoa, you grew this – can you grow this?' And I said, 'Well, I'll give it a shot.' So it just snowballed from there." Over the years, Rob has learned or developed many techniques to germinate seed where others have failed (or failed to try).

Rob's annual harvest has proven indispensible to Chicago-region restorations. In the early years, stewards began to realize that certain native species were hardly represented in restorations. The seeds were rarely collected, and when they were, volunteers weren't finding many. The late Citizens for Conservation steward, Tom Vanderpoel, collected only about a half-dozen prairie phlox seeds in his 30-plus years of restoration work, and not for lack of trying.

Most of these hard-to-collect species were diminutive, hiding beneath other plants or duff.

Rob Sulski's backyard seed garden.
(His front yard, full of woodland natives, isn't bad either.)

Many were ephemeral, appearing just a few weeks each spring, their seed harvestable during only a brief window each year. Volunteers had to be there after the seed was ripe and before the plant ejected it or it otherwise dispersed. Even when seed for these species did manage to be sown, the amounts were miniscule.

The need for such locally sourced conservative seeds and plugs in restorations is great. Most landscaping companies don't offer these species, given the low commercial demand and difficulty in rearing them. When they are available, the price can be prohibitive, especially for the hundreds of sites where they're needed, and numerous questions about provenance and genetics arise.

While Rob isn't the only one doing this work in the region, there's plenty of room for others to join in. "A lot of stuff, I end up doing by default, because no one else is doing it," says Rob. "That motivates me, though, once I get into it. Once you start doing it and start whistling, and you get results that kind of blow your own mind, it's almost like fishing. That's why people keep fishing. They cast and cast and then they get that one, and it compels them to keep fishing."

Gallery of the Overlooked

Give these little plants their due.

Some native plants vie for attention. Others live in relative obscurity — and often get overlooked in restorations.

Many of the species on the following pages, all of which Rob has grown, don't get much taller than six inches. Blooming only briefly in the spring or early summer, they hide beneath the dessicated remains of last year's prairies and woods, and their seeds are difficult to collect in the wild.

Yet these delicate plants are essential components of high-quality ecosystems. Among other benefits, they support a multitude of ants, bees, and other insects before the high-summer flush of blooms takes hold.

For restorations to be as complete as possible, consider encouraging these and other native early seeders, whether by seeding or planting them as plugs.

PRAIRIE
Full sun,
moderate
to dry soil

Prairie Violet

Viola pedatifida

With a pale-purple flower and finely divided leaves, this violet is a study in understated grace. "It's an early seeder," says Rob, "but it keeps shooting up pods all summer. By then, though, the plant has disappeared under the prairie matrix." This makes it especially worthwhile to keep in a home garden setting, where it will produce much better with limited competition.

Collect: May – August

Tips: "When the pod starts turning up before a storm event, that's when you get them into a bucket and get the screen over them." Keep an eye on violets into fall, when they may give a surprise second bloom.

Prairie Phlox

Phlox pilosa fulgida

Found in both dry and moist prairie remnants, prairie phlox makes a bold impression growing in swaths of pink, turning blue toward the end of the bloom. Rob propagates two other genus members as well: marsh phlox (*Phlox glaberrima interior*) and the more common – but still hard to collect – woodland phlox (*Phlox divaricata*).

Collect: June – July

Tips: Grow these like the violets, in a dedicated pot (see p. 36). After the last bloom, usually the third week of June, put a nylon stocking over them, secured with a twist tie ("bag 'em," in Rob's words). Give them a month, then clip off the whole thing – stem, stocking, and seeds.

PRAIRIE, SAVANNA
Dry soil

Yellow Star Grass

Hypoxis hirsuta

An unabashed fuzzy ray of brightness shining through last year's dull tangle of duff, *Hypoxis* brightens the muddy domain of prairie crayfish in high-quality grasslands.

Collect: mid-June – mid-July

Tips: *Hypoxis* will do best in a dedicated, well-weeded garden, either by itself or with blue-eyed grass. In early summer, the plant forms seed capsules. "It's hard to tell when it's ripe," says Rob. "You have to get on your hands and knees." The capsules will plump and perforate, and then the top half of the sepal splits, "and they pour out in a hurry." To avoid missing it, pick the capsule as soon as it gets a little translucent. "The flower stem grows out three times the length of its leaves, then folds over and hugs the ground," says Rob. "It's their method of dispersing."

PRAIRIE
Full to part sun,
moderate to dry soil

Violet Wood Sorrel

Oxalis violacea

The three leaflets of violet wood sorrel give it the same delicate shamrock look as its ubiquitous, weedy relative, *Oxalis stricta*, but with violet-pink blooms instead of yellow.

Collect: A two-week period between June 1 and July 1

Tips: Rob grows *Oxalis* in dedicated pots. "You get a lot of seedheads," he says. "Collect them when they pale out. Otherwise, they split and drop rapidly. You can take a pot at a time at the picnic table and clip off the ones that are getting white. Each half-week, I grab a plant."

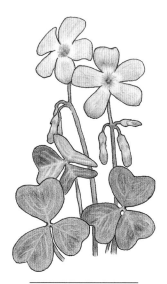

PRAIRIE, WOODS
Full to part sun,
moderate to dry soil

PRAIRIE
Full sun,
dry soil

Prairie Skullcap

Scutellaria leonardii

You'd be forgiven for overlooking the beauty of this miniature prairie dweller, which can be as short as three inches. But get up close and admire the purple filigree adorning the little flower, a cross between a foxglove trumpet and the scoop of a classic muscle car.

Collect: mid-June – mid-August

Tips: "I leave them in small pots," says Rob. The seed capsule is unique: "It's a spoon with a flat cap. The cap peels off, and the seeds spill out." To collect the seed, Rob turns the pot sideways, holding the plant over a bowl, and pulls the caps. He does three or four rounds of this during the collection period. "To try to do that in the wild," he says, "would be a pain in the butt."

Leiberg's Panic Grass

Dichanthelium leibergii

When it comes to cool-season grasses, stewards focus a lot of attention on the invasives they're trying to remove. But there's a whole suite of desirable cool-season grasses, from porcupine, vanilla, and June grasses to conservative panic grasses. Steward Stephen Packard calls Leiberg's "one of the most characteristic species of high-quality prairie." Its presence usually signals a remnant. At least one study has shown that grassland birds prefer nesting in remnants with panic grass to restorations without it.

Collect: late June – mid-July.

PRAIRIE
Full sun,
dry soil

False Dandelion

Krigia biflora

Also known as two-flowered Cynthia, *Krigia* can reach almost two feet in height. It doesn't hide like most of the others in this list, but its seeds are liable to float away on the wind, uncollected. It does quite well without competition.

Collect: June – September

Tips: Seedwise, *Krigia* acts a lot like common dandelion, says Rob, though it produces many fewer seeds. "It flowers over a month and a half. Seeds very quickly flare out like dandelion. It closes after blooming, the sepals flare open, and you see fluff." Collecting twice a day will maximize your harvest.

PRAIRIE, SAVANNA
Full or part sun,
wet to dry soil

Fire Pink

Silene virginica

Fire pink – the name evokes passion and intrigue, perhaps a flamenco dancer. And this wildflower doesn't disappoint, with five bright cardinal-red rays, each tipped with two flamboyant lobes. Fire pink does well in shady suburban yards, though some stewards report having trouble establishing it by seed in restorations.

Collect: mid-June

Tips: Just as with phlox and violets, Rob uses the "nylon stocking method" for fire pink (see page 37). Pull the stocking over the seedheads in early July, when the last flower petals wilt. Clip around the third week of July, give or take a week.

WOODS
Part sun, moderate
to wet soil

Stout Blue-Eyed Grass

Sisyrhinchium angustifolium

This unassuming little iris is a pleasure to find in some remote patch of prairie or a sun-dappled savanna, especially if you catch it in bloom. Though small, the clean, deep electric blue blooms accented with gold stick in the memory. "The flowering stems grow much longer than the leaves," says Rob, "and fold over quite a distance." *S. albidum* and the state-endangered *S. montanum* are also well worth propagating.

Collect: July 15 – August 15

Tips: "The seeds ripen over time," says Rob. "Wait until the capsules turn brown -- don't pick the green ones. As soon as they change, pick them before they split open and drop the seeds."

PRAIRIE, SAVANNA
Full or part sun,
wet to dry soil

Pennsylvania Sedge
Carex pensylvanica

Penn sedge is common in our oak woodlands and savannas. That said, it's an essential matrix species in restorations, so it's a sought-after species for propagation. It also forms a mat that looks great as groundcover in shady yards.

Collect: mid-June

Tips: Collecting Penn sedge seed is difficult, and seeding this species into restorations hasn't been very successful. Spreading well by rhizomes, it may be best introduced as plugs created by dividing up mature plants. Growing from seed isn't impossible, though. "The trick there — and also with cool-season grasses — is to get the seed in flats right away and keep the flats damp," says Rob.

SAVANNA
Full sun,
wet soil

Shooting Star
Dodecatheon meadia

What is shooting star, that oft-photographed darling of spring prairies, doing in a list of overlooked species? According to steward Stephen Packard, 90 percent of restorations don't have it. It's also a gorgeous addition to a sunny seed garden.

Collect: early to mid-July

Tips: Shooting star is extremely easy to grow by seed, so seed grown in gardens will give a lot of bang for the buck out in the field. You can throw seed directly into a restoration with great results, but it also retains viability in a fall seed mix.

PRAIRIE, SAVANNA
Full or part sun,
wet to dry soil

Selections here are largely upland, mesic habitats, most often the subjects of volunteer efforts. For more plants in need of propagation, see pages 44 and 45. Plants not shown to scale. Collection dates are for Rob's yard. Your microclimate may vary.

A Hard-Working Yard

Rob Sulski has turned his yard into a nursery for uncommon plants. Here's a peek at the annual ebb and flow of a propagation operation.

❶ Prep and Set Out Flats
In early April, blow the autumn leaves off the previous year's plants and set them out. Remove seeds from stratification and spread in germination flats – in late March for seeds that need a "cool" cycle, third week of April for those that don't. Place flats in partial sun, if possible – full sun can dry out even prairie species. Always make sure the soil stays moist.

❷ Watch Early Seeders
Grow a separate garden, in pots or in the ground, dedicated to plants that bloom before July 4. (Without competition, they'll produce more seed and will be easier to see.) Put them somewhere you can water them and keep a close eye for the often-brief seed collection windows, mostly during May and June. If collecting seed for a restoration, some species must get on site right away.

❸ Transfer Plants To Pots
As seedlings mature through early summer, they'll need new homes. Volunteers first descend on Rob's picnic table in late May to transplant spring ephemerals into larger cells and plug pots. The process repeats as later-emerging plants become ready.

❹ Include Later-Season Species

Rob cares for a range of rare plants, which bloom and set seed at various times of year. Where possible, he groups these according to bloom time to make it easier to monitor and collect seed. Rob often pairs multiple community members – such as *Carex bicknellii*, *Asclepias tuberosa*, and *Zizia aptera* – in a single container, mostly to save room. Keep watering, especially seedlings and plants in pots.

❺ Late Bloomers

By early fall, about three-quarters of seedlings have matured enough for outplanting or have had their seed collected. Some, though, need multiple years to reach outplanting stage, perhaps requiring more than one cold-warm cycle to germinate. Give them more time and keep them from drying out.

❻ Keep Collecting Seed

Rob's front and back yards are full of native perennial beds, which provide a low-maintenance, recurring source of seeds, as well as decor and enjoyment. The plantings also contribute to the overall vitality of the garden by attracting pollinators and enriching the environment.

❼ Put Flats To Bed

Around November, move any remaining active flats to a corner of the yard. Lay a permeable fabric barrier on them, and rake fall leaves over that in preparation for overwintering. If you plan on germinating seeds next year, start them on a stratification regime or get them in soil and leave out in the elements.

The Setup

Here's what you need to put together a starter seed operation — either a few potted plants or a germination flat.

Space

The space you need depends on your ambition. Rob's roughly 60- by 100-foot yard allows him to grow thousands of plants, but all you really need to start is open space for a few pots.

Supplies

If you garden at all, you've probably got most of what you need already.

- trowel or small shovel

- garden hose or watering can

- table fork

- 1 plastic germination flat (10" x 14") and two or three 2.25" x 2.25" x 4" form pots with trays

- large bin, bucket, tarp, or wheelbarrow, for mixing soil

- 3–5 lbs soil mix (see recipe, opposite) Shortcut: use off-the-shelf potting soil

- 2–3 mature native plants, or seed

- optional: porous fabric vegetation barrier for overwintering plants

- optional: wood planks and cinder blocks to build racks for multiple germination flats or pots (inhibits ants and slugs)

- optional: several larger pots

- optional: large plastic bin for soaking transplants

No yard? No problem! Even conservative natives can be grown on an apartment balcony or in a side yard.

Soil Mix Recipe

Use this multipurpose mix for transplanting plugs or germinating seeds.

The chances of success are highest if you have a well-aerated, high-nutrient soil that holds moisture. Rob uses this mix for everything, in pots, flats, and garden plots. (Makes 45 lbs of soil, good for about six form-pot flats.)

In large container (e.g., wheelbarrow), mix*:

1 40 lb. bag of Michigan Mix soil

"It's black, loamy soil with some fine sand in there," says Rob.

2 to 3 qts. peat moss

"I'd like to substitute more sustainable shredded coir (coconut fiber), but I'd have to experiment with that. You need something to hold onto the moisture. Otherwise you're out there watering three times a day."

2 to 3 qts. torpedo sand

"It's patio flat paver sand, which is courser than sandbox sand. I get it at the hardware store."

*Rob filters out sticks and rocks using a screen, then blends the mixture with his hands. "We put our spirit into the soil," he says.

A Few Dirty Tricks

- If you're growing a plant for more than one season, says Rob, sprinkle a little agricultural lime on top of the soil. Constant watering can leach out nutrients and leave the soil acidic. Lime restores pH balance.

- You can reuse soil, too. "At the end of the year," he says, "I mix the old soil into new, prepared soil."

How to Start Growing Rare Seed

Sure, you can propagate plants from seed, using stratification and other treatments (see pages 38 and 39). But you can also just begin with a few outdoor plants and let nature do most of the work. Here's an easy way to get started.

1.   Choose species and home site.

Figure out what to grow based on conservation need, availability of plants, and the growing space you have. Find a patch of earth with the right moisture and sun, or a good place outdoors for potted plants. The key is to choose easy-to-monitor spots where you'll see them often.

2.   Get some plants.

Get at least three individual plants so they can pollinate each other. Having more plants attracts and sustains pollinator populations, and accounts for some plants dying. See page 40 for more sourcing tips.

3. Plant them.

When you plant or re-pot, try to keep as much original soil around your plants' roots as possible. If planting in spring, plant the top of the plug flush with surface. In fall, plant an inch deeper to compensate for frost heaving.

4.   Nurture your babies.

Check daily and keep moist. If you go on vacation, get a plantsitter. Mature plants may produce seed the first year, but seedlings may have to be nurtured for a few years.

5.   Collect seed.

When seeds start forming, check your plant at least daily — the collection window can be very narrow (or quite long). Some seed ejects (see box), while other seed can be clipped or pulled by hand. You can sow seed right away. (For some early seeders, it's a must.)

To Catch Sneaky Seeds

Rob's technique for capturing ejected violet seed also works for *phlox* and other species: "Put the pot inside a five-gallon pail and put a screen over it. Then as those seeds explode, they're in the pail or the pot, and I just take a spoon and get them out. If I want to grow those violets, I leave the ones that fell into the pot in there, sprinkle a little soil on them; each time, more seed goes on. And then I overwinter those pots under leaves in the yard and pull them out in the spring. You'll have hundreds of little violets growing. I've tried sowing those seeds in a separate germination flat — you only get a tenth the amount."

Rob also captures seed using hosiery: "Once the near-the-last flower is done, I just bundle 'em up, put the nylon stocking over them and close it with a bread tie."

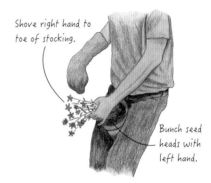

Shove right hand to toe of stocking.

Bunch seed heads with left hand.

Grasp top of bunch with stocking hand, then use left hand to peel sock over bunch. Twist-tie stocking against stem below seed heads.

6. Want more seed?

Germinate new plants that will make their own! Sow seed beneath the plant that produced it (see box) and allow the parent plants' soil microbes to work their magic.

7. How about plugs?

When seedlings are 1–3" tall, they're ready to "fork out." Transplant into form pots, rapping to settle the soil. The first time you water, do it from beneath (Rob soaks the whole flat in a plastic bin), then gently. Keeping plants into the next growing season will give them the best chance of survival when you outplant.

An Introduction to Propagation Techniques

Get more seed, faster.

To better grow plants from seed, a host of techniques mimic the way outdoor conditions break down seed coats and stimulate germination. Rob favors these often involved processes because they can save space, time, and produce more seed and plugs. Here's a primer.

Stratification

Storing seeds at specific moistures and temperatures for set periods of time — called "stratification" because the process can involve layering — simulates ideal dormancy conditions and gives the grower more control than relying on weather. "The fridge gives more assurance that treatment will occur," says Rob. (He keeps two refrigerator drawers at 33° F, measured with a thermometer.)

Different species require different regimes. For instance, most late seeders (plants that drop seed after July 10) need a straightforward cold-moist regime, meaning seeds spend 90 days in a baggie of moist soil in Rob's garage fridge before being planted outside. Other plants, especially early seeders, need warm-moist followed by cold-moist regimes. Double stratification (cold-warm-cold-warm) combines regimes for species that need multiple seasons to germinate, such as many early woodland plants. As we said, it can get complex!

Dry Stratification

Keep seed loose in a bag or envelope, and keep rodents away.

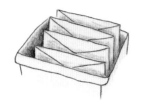

Moist Stratification

Mix seeds into moist substrate (sand or soil) in a baggie. Check weekly for mold, drying, and sprouting.

Scarification

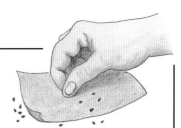

Many hard-seeded species germinate better if their seed coats are scratched or lightly abraded. (Broad-leaved puccoon and columbine are two.) A brownie tin in his lap, and preferably watching "stupid movies," Rob pulls each tiny seed by hand over fine sandpaper. At least part of each seed should go "from shiny to dull."

Inoculation

Some seedlings need specific microbes for ideal growth. You can buy inoculant, but the easiest way to include microbes is to mix in soil from around the roots of a mature plant or grow the seed under a parent. While there's some debate over the efficacy of inoculation, Rob says it aids in growing most legumes and possibly other plant families.

Hot Water

New Jersey tea likes a hot bath. Rob first lightly scarifies the seeds, then pours a cup of hot water over them. Once it cools, he drains the water and places the seeds into stratification.

Fire

To germinate *Geranium bicknellii*, Rob built a brick hearth on a concrete slab, laid down soil and seeds—then leaves, sticks, and charcoal—fired it up, and let the seeds bake for an hour at 100 °F. Then he threw the cooled soil into a flat to overwinter.

Learn More

The Tallgrass Restoration Handbook (Packard, Mutel)
Prairie Moon Nursery's Seed Treatment Table (prairiemoon.com)

Thoughts on Sourcing

Where to get plants or seeds.

How does one responsibly obtain plants or seeds to propagate for restoration? The best person to contact is often the steward of your local natural area. Working with the landowner, the steward will likely know what species are needed most, as well as what source material may be available.

If you're just going to care for plants and collect their seed, those plants may most easily and sustainably come from another volunteer's seed garden or from a native plant sale, often organized by conservation organizations. (Make sure those plants are appropriately sourced, and avoid native cultivars). Occasionally, plants are rescued from remnant acreages or plantings about to succumb to a bulldozer. If you're going the seed route, a steward may also share seed collected by volunteers.

When in doubt, err on the side of caution and follow the lead of stewards, preserve staff, and landowners.

On Genes

Part of what restorations preserve is the diversity of genotypes that evolved in microhabitats across the landscape. Much research recommends that seed come from near a restoration site, although that choice is complicated by both the source and recipient site's quality and other factors, to say nothing of the need to adapt for climate change. For more, consult the Forest Preserves of Cook County Seed Source Policy and Guidelines.

To prevent crossing with cultivars or plants of unknown provenance, avoid having other plants of the same species growing in the garden, unless they are natives that originated close to the recipient restoration.

Rules & Regs

It's illegal to take plants or plant material (seeds, etc.) from forest preserves and nature preserves without permission. That goes for adding seed or plants, too. Always consult with the landowner and steward before collecting, seeding, or planting anything.

Keeping Track

For those who like to geek out over spreadsheets.

Species	Trtmnt Regime	Strat. Time, Total Days	Sun	Wet Cat.	Wet Rank	Seed Collect Date	Seed Source	Local/Non	Warm Dry storage	Cold dry storage (11/25/16)	Start Date	W (70)	Star Date
Andropogon scoparius	C(0)				4	9/30-10/29/16	Soo,NAS,Foss	L		x			
Anemone canadensis	CWCW				2	?	CFC	N	x		?		
Anemonella thalictroides												Over-seeded into Steve 2014 flat	
	WCW Fresh Flat				5	?	Jane	L			?-7/29/16		7/29
Angelica atropurpurea	CWCW		5	OBL	1	?	Steve-SPG	L	x		?		
Aralia racemosa	C(60), Fall Flat				5	?	Steve	L		x			
Arenaria lateriflora	WCW Baggie, surface				5	?	Jane	L				Baggie w/PANLAT	7/30
Asclepias purpurascens	C(105)				4	10/9-11/11/16	Garden	L		x			
Asclepias tuberosa	C(105)				5	9/30/16 (late)	Soo	L		x			
Aster macrophyllus	C(120)				5	10/17-28/16	Steve,Home,Ch	L		x			
Aster puniceus	C(60)					10/29/16	Foss	L		x			
Baptisia leucopheae	C(30),scar, inoc		5	UPL	5	7/28-8/15/2016	GBN	L		x			
Beckmannia schyzigachne	C(60), cool		5	OBL	1	7/16/16	Steve-SPG	L		x			
Blephilia hirsuta	C(60),surface sow			FACU-	4	?	Steve-SW	L		x			
Brachyelytrum erectum	C(30?),Cool		2	UPL	5	?	Steve-SPG	L		x			
Carex tuckermanii	C(60)Cool		3	OBL	1	?	Steve	L		x			
Castilleja coccinea	C(60),surface sow				3	6/16/16	Steve-SPG	L	x				
Caulophyllum thalictroides	WCWC				5	8/6-12/16	Steve,Home	L		x			
Chelone glabra	C(120)				1	10/28/16	Ch	L		x			
Commandra umbulatum	Fresh w/host				4	6/7/16	Steve, Tyner	L			?	Fresh w/SPHINT& ANDSCO Plugs	8/15
Delphinium tricorne	C(60)				5	5/28/16	Normal, IL	N		x			
Desmodium cuspidatum	C(0),dehusk,inoc			UPL	5	?	Steve	L		x			
Desmodium glutinosum	C(10),dehusk,inoc			UPL	5	?	Steve	L		x			
Dicentra cucullaria	WCW Fresh Flat				5	5/9/16	Varble	L			5/9/16	x	5/21
Dodecatheon meadii	WCW Fresh Flat				4	6/21-7/10/16	Home, GBN	L		x			
Echinacea pallida	C(90)				5	10/29/16	Foss	L		x			
Euonymous atropurpureus	WCW			FAC-	3	?	Steve	L		x			90	1/10
Euphorbia corollata	C(30)		5	UPL	5	?	Steve	L		x			
Galium circaezans hypomalacum	C(60)				5	?	Jane	L		x			
Gentiana andrewsii	C(60),surface sow				2	9/29-?/16	319,Soo	L		x			
Gentiana puberulenta	C(60),surface sow				5	10/14-?/16	GBN	L		x			
Helianthus rigidus	C(60)				5	9/30-10/14/16	Soo,GBN	L		x			
Hepatica acutiloba												Over-seeded fresh into Steve 2016 flat	
	WCW Fresh Flat				5	?	Jane	L		x			7/29

A snapshot of Rob's detailed database. (We couldn't fit all 32 columns on this page.)

Rob keeps a detailed spreadsheet that tracks everything from a species' seed requirements to dates for each treatment regime. He also records where his seeds or plants have come from and when they were collected. That provenance helps determine how they should be used in a restoration.

Rob's comments column helps him strategize: "Did this work? Didn't it work? What does Prairie Moon say? What does Tom Clothier say about growing these seeds? What does some other research say? What did I find is best? What I've found is best, that's the regime I use in the future."

To tailor your approach and learn from mistakes (and because it's fun), you can also keep phenological records of bloom time and seed set, as well as yield and germination rate.

Outplanting

Begin with the end in mind.

Before you begin propagating, know where seed will go. Make sure it's needed and part of the landholder's plan. "We have limited habitat for *V. pedatifida* in Lake County," says Kelly Schultz of the Lake County Forest Preserves, "but we have an abundance of places to add *Polemonium reptans* and *Oxalis violacea*, and so much *Trillium grandiflorum* that we don't need to add seed or plants."

Many stewards already have a good idea of where they're trying to establish populations. Make sure you're communicating with recipients of your seeds or plugs so they're ready when the seeds are and can tend any new plantings, watering until the dormant season, if possible.

The end goal, in a sense, is to move most seed production from the yard into the wild. "The best success," says Kelly, "comes from establishing small plots in the wild that could be collected and spread on their own."

Some stewards plant plugs in triangles to better identify introductions and whether they're taking.

On Sowing Early Seeders

"A lot of early seeders need to get in the soil right away," says Rob. "So if you collect them, store them, and wait for a seed cleaning, their viability is already diminishing with each day as they dry out. In the wild, they explode and land on the soil and then keep moist. If you collect *Phlox* or *Hypoxis* or *Viola pedatifida*, you can let them dry out for a week, but clean them right away, get them in damp soil, and keep them damp. And then, when it comes time to sow seeds in the wild, just add those bags to the mixes." You can also just spread them on your site immediately after collecting.

To the Neighborhoods!

The more gardens, the better.

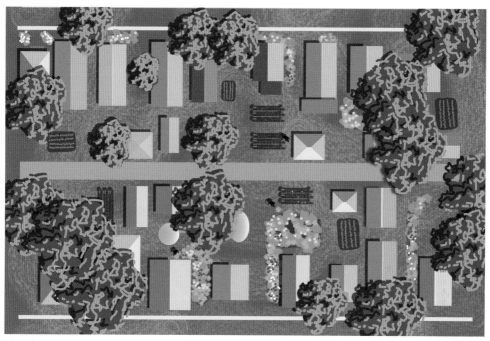

Your block? Blossoms spring through fall, neighbors sharing seed (and tomatoes), habitat for birds and butterflies, and a powerhouse producer of rare plants for the local preserve.

What would it mean to get many more volunteer seed gardens up and running throughout Chicago Wilderness? "If we had a thousand yards producing *Hypoxis* seed, or *Phlox pilosa*, or *Baptisia leucophaea*, restorations could certainly use it all," says steward Stephen Packard.

A network of gardens wouldn't just mean many times the number of rare plants available for restorations. It would mean a wave of folks gaining expertise with largely overlooked species, yards growing in diversity and potentially supporting an increasing array of wildlife.

What's most needed now, says Stephen, are more successful models, with well-coordinated gardens supplying well-managed plantings and gaining the confidence of more land managers.

One such model is the Wild Seed Garden Project, a network started by the North Branch Restoration Project in 1985. North Branch garden coordinator Gayle Laboda reports that, as of 2020, the North Branch has 38 gardens growing 190 species, including many rare or endangered species. "The Wild Gardeners nurture and enjoy the plants in their gardens," she says, "and the seed gets planted in North Branch sites."

The Next Frontier

So many challenges, so little time.

Seed propagation is a work in progress. For some species, Rob has had only intermittent success and says the process could be improved. For others, he's still scratching his head. Can you crack the code?

False toadflax
(and other hemi-parasites)

Comandra umbellata

Rob succeeded early on by plugging seed in with hosts such as wedge grass, phlox, dropseed, and little bluestem. But subsequent batches have produced far fewer seedlings. Indian paintbrush is another tough hemi-parasite. "I got some seeds twice, but I just didn't get anything out of them."

Prairie lily
Lilium philadelphicum

Rob assumed prairie lilies needed double stratifcation, but eventually found a few years in the yard works best. He's gotten hundreds of seedlings using cold stratification, but none have survived transplanting.

Blue cohosh
Caulophyllum thalictroides

"I haven't been able to grow any using various methods. It may need to go through the gut of mammals or birds." One method he's considering is using a pre-treatment of gibberelic acid.

White trillium
(and other woodland species)

Trillium grandiflorum

Plants such as trillium, twinleaf, yellow dog-toothed violet, bellwort, and hepatica require as many as seven years to bloom from seed. Rob has been able to compress that using multiple 60-day stratification periods, but it still takes years. "How many days are really necessary?" he asks.

Gentians

"The seeds are so tiny," says Rob. "They need to be surface-sowed. They need UV light to break down the seed coat. They need protection from the weather, and need to be watered from below." The crux: devise ways to lessen disruption of the seeds.

Orchids

Rob has only dabbled with orchids. "That's a whole other — it's a laboratory process."

The Sought-After 60

Stewards Tom and Jim Vanderpoel created this list of plants they wished were in their restorations. While Rob grows many of them, there's no shortage of species for which seeds and plugs are needed.*

Agalinus auriculata
Agropyron trachycaulum
Apocynum androsaemifolium
Asclepius sullivantii
Astragalus canadensis
Athyrium filix-femina michauxii
Baptisia leucophaea
Brachyelytrum erectum
Calystegia spithamaea
Campanula aparinoides
Carex interior
Caulophyllum thalictroides
Comarum palustre
Dichanthelium boreale
Dichanthelium latifolium
Dichanthelium leibergii
Erigeron pulchellus
Galium obtusum
Galium tinctorium
Linum sulcatum
Liparis liliifolia
Lysimachia lanceolata
Micranthes pensylvanica
Muhlenbergia glomerata
Muhlenbergia sylvatica
Piptatherum racemosum
Panax quinquefolium
Perideridia americana
Phlox divaricata
Phlox glaberrima
Poa palustris
Polygala verticillata
Polytaenia nuttallii

Ranunculus flabellaris
Rosa palustris
Rosa setigera tomentosa
Rumex verticillatus
Salix humilis
Schoenoplectus acutus
Silene virginica
Sisyrinchium angustifolium
Smilacina stellata
Solidago patula
Sparganium emersum
Sphenopholis intermedia
Spiraea alba
Spiranthes magnicamporum
Symplocarpus foetidus
Stellaria longifolia
Thaspium trifoliatum
Thelypteris palustris
Trillium flexipes
Turritis glabra
Utricularia macrorhiza
Vallisneria americana
Vicia caroliniana
Viola labradorica
Viola pedatifida
Viola pubescens
Zizia aptera

*This list is for Citizens for Conservation's Barrington-area sites. "Sought-after" lists for other areas may look quite different.

Notes

About Rob Sulski

With a bachelor's in zoology and ecology and a master's in environmental engineering, Rob Sulski made his way to the Illinois Environmental Protection Agency, where he worked for 28 years in water pollution control before starting his own nature restoration and management company, Footstone, Inc.

Rob's volunteer career began even earlier. The forest preserves have been part of his life since grade school. "I lived on Chipilly Woods," he says. "I actually would dig up plants from there and bring them to my parents' house and plant them." (Please don't do this now, advises the older, wiser Rob.) At Glenbrook North High School in the mid-1960s, Rob studied under Marion Cole, who managed and studied several local natural areas, including Glenbrook North Prairie. "She had a desk in the greenhouse," says Rob. "I was given an opportunity to get out of silent study hall if I wanted to assist her."

After college, Rob got involved in the North Branch Restoration Project and took over stewardship of Glenbrook North Prairie, where he's been ever since. North Branch stewards soon caught wind of how Rob was propagating seed for Glenbrook, and the rest is history.

Rob has been a falconer since 1968 and has conducted fall migrant raptor research for decades. "I trap, band, and salvage feathers from peregrines for stable isotope analysis," he says. Rob also sings and plays harmonica and guitar in two local bands. He restored the Glenview house he and his wife bought as a "handyman's special," where they raised four kids — and did a little gardening besides.

Reclaiming
Sedge Meadow

with Tom Vanderpoel

---

*Many a sedge meadow restoration has slid back into a mess of reed canary grass.
That was before the ten warriors.*

Around 2010, landscaper Tom Vanderpoel, a leader with the volunteer group Citizens for Conservation (CFC), was out on a workday. Pulling sweet clover in the prairie at Flint Creek Savanna in Barrington, Illinois, he kept finding himself scanning along the creek, thirty or forty feet down below. "Inside this big floodplain I could see the tiny little pockets of sedge meadow, partially overrun with reed canary. And I started thinking, 'How does that stuff stay there?'" What was it about these native sedges, he wondered, that had allowed them to hold out for over a century against exotic plant invaders?

Low, wet, sometimes difficult to access, sedge meadows are an underappreciated habitat. Very few people have managed to successfully restore them. CFC had tried before and failed. They'd first attacked relatively large acreages of reed canary grass, herbiciding about three acres at once. "It's very easy to kill reed canary and so we did it, and then we put sedges in," says Tom. "We might've had a follow-up or two, and

then we would go on to the next place." But over the next five years, the volunteers found invasives returning in force. "It seems like I'm wasting effort and time," Tom thought. "And should the sedge meadow have been stronger by now?"

That's when Tom started noticing those sedges. "I started thinking maybe we should use those spots as a beachhead, to try to restore bigger areas. And so that's what we did. We first went right over the top of the existing sedge meadow and other remnant plants and killed reed canary using, at that time, Poast. Poast only targets grasses, and if there were native grasses in it—and there is some bluejoint in there—they would be vulnerable, but all the sedges and forbs would be okay. And so we went over the top, and, much to our glee, it really pounded the reed canary. And with one burn, all of a sudden, those sedges that hadn't had any attention in 100 years started to really flourish.... From that spot, we started to advance."

Before we dive into how to restore a sedge meadow, it helps to know how to read some of the features of one.

Anatomy of a Sedge Meadow
(through Tom V's eyes)

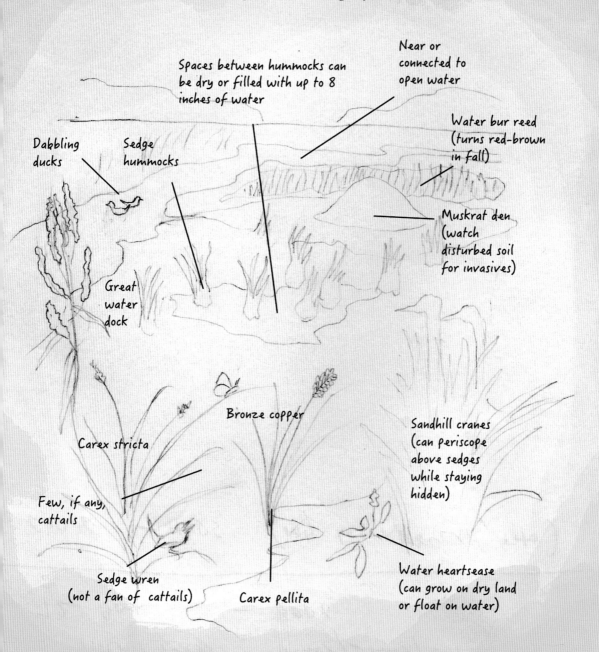

Spaces between hummocks can be dry or filled with up to 8 inches of water

Near or connected to open water

Water bur reed (turns red-brown in fall)

Dabbling ducks

Sedge hummocks

Muskrat den (watch disturbed soil for invasives)

Great water dock

Bronze copper

Sandhill cranes (can periscope above sedges while staying hidden)

Carex stricta

Few, if any, cattails

Sedge wren (not a fan of cattails)

Carex pellita

Water heartsease (can grow on dry land or float on water)

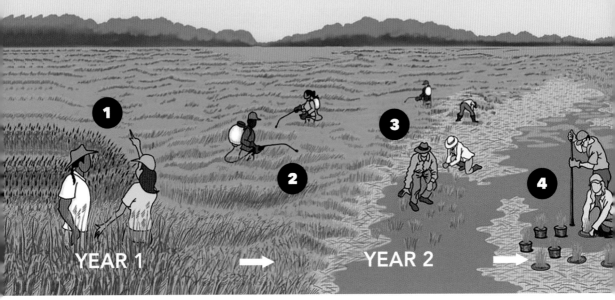

Many sedge meadows are in poor shape. Success requires careful site selection and an intense opening salvo.

Follow-up is critical. After the spring herbiciding, plant sedges, followed by another spray treatment.

YEAR 1 → YEAR 2 →

The Sedge Meadow Sequence

Tom Vanderpoel developed this successful recipe for restoring sedge meadows, though he says there's plenty of room for improvement.

❶ Identify Site
Locate remnants, if any exist, and focus on expanding them, ideally connecting two. Size of restoration should match resources for long-term follow-through. Create a restoration plan now, and source the seed you'll need in step 6.

❷ Herbicide
Early summer of year one, overspray the restoration area to eliminate reed canary grass and phragmites. Use grass-selective herbicide in areas where native sedges and forbs persist. (Per the label, you can only spray when the wetland is dry.) In completely overrun areas, use a general aquatic herbicide. Hand wick cattails and purple loosestrife. Spray and wick again in late summer. Observe site three times a week and treat as needed. The goal by fall: no signs of living invasives.

❸ Spray And Pull
In spring of year two, spray for missed invasive plants and resprouts (especially reed canary, which will come back vigorously). Pull cattail shoots.

❹ Plant The Warriors
After spring spraying (mid-May to June), plant plugs of the "ten warrior sedges" (page 52) in a grid. Aim for three feet apart, but plant as densely as budget allows. "The object is to get the sedges to merge and form a matrix," says Tom. "The farther apart those sedges are, the more vulnerable you are." Planting plugs too late (after late August or so) risks them being upturned by frost heaving.

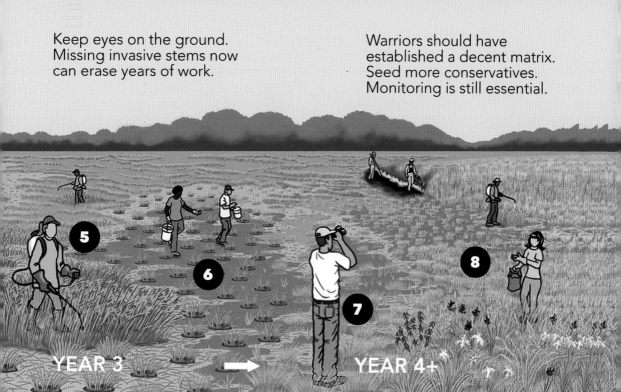

Keep eyes on the ground.
Missing invasive stems now
can erase years of work.

Warriors should have
established a decent matrix.
Seed more conservatives.
Monitoring is still essential.

YEAR 3

YEAR 4+

❺ Spray Again

In late summer of year two, spray invasive resprouts with a grass-selective herbicide. "Don't rush out right away when you see the first ones—let the full crop show up," says Tom. Return for missed ones later in fall. "Reed canary stands out like a sore thumb," he says. "When the natives start to go brown, it's green."

❻ Seed Natives

Hand sow native forbs and sedges before Thanksgiving. Leave grasses out of the mix for now, since they can become victims to your follow-up herbiciding. Seed in as much diversity as you can find—at least 40 species, across as many seasons and families as possible. Beginning a regular prescribed fire regimen helps burn off duff for spot spraying and encourages native seedlings.

❼ Remain Vigilant

In year three, monitor your site for new outbreaks. Reed canary may continue to appear for five years or more, and new seed may come from upstream. Inspect site at least two times a year (early and late season). Spot herbicide.

❽ Keep Hunting And Seeding

Repeat steps 6 and 7 for at least three years. By now your sedge matrix should have filled in. Continue seeding in conservative forbs and sedges. Continue monitoring for as long as possible. While this could extend 20 or more years, it may only take one well-trained volunteer going out a few times a year. Most importantly, never turn your back on even a well-established site.

The Ten Warrior Sedges

Dark-Scaled
Sedge
Carex buxbaumii

Broad-Leaved
Wooly Sedge
Carex pellita

Running Marsh
Sedge
Carex sartwellii

Riverbank
Sedge
Carex emoryi

Hairy-Fruited
Lake Sedge
Carex trichocarpa

Hairy-Leaved
Lake Sedge
Carex atherodes

Common
Lake Sedge
Carex lacustris

Common Yellow
Lake Sedge
Carex utriculata

Common
Tussock Sedge
Carex stricta

Long-Bracted
Tussock Sedge
Carex aquatilis

These sedges are CFC's field-tested tool for holding ground during restoration until conservatives can take root. Sedges preferring wetter conditions are toward the bottom. You can experiment with placement, since most sedges will move by rhizomes to find optimal moisture.

Enlisting the Ten Warriors

By Tom Vanderpoel

We didn't just pick any old sedges for our sedge meadow restorations. We have what's known as the "ten warriors." When we first picked them, I didn't particularly focus on their function in a restoration. We picked them because they were dominant in remnant sedge meadows. But then, the function proved so important. Almost all of these sedges move on rhizomes, so when we plant them in the grid pattern, they will start to merge together. One 2" x 2" plug can have four to six little sedges starting to come up all around it, and they're moving out four to five inches every year. In two to three to four years, depending on how far apart you plant them, they're going to seal it up and establish your matrix.

The ten warrior sedges are aggressive enough to have survived out in sedge meadow remnants with no management for 100 years. If they can do that, particularly without burning, that's telling me something. We've seen *Carex stricta* and *Carex pellita* and *Carex lacustris* and some of these others just desperately hanging on without any help. What we're also seeing is that after six or seven years of intense management, they and the forbs are now dominating.

What's more, they don't appear to box out any of the delicate forbs. My guess is that they're actually protecting them. These forbs know how to grow with the ten warriors. They've evolved together for 10,000 years or more. We've seen the same thing in savannas and prairies. In prairies, where dropseed is dominant, it gets hold and keeps out other grasses. But that doesn't stop plants like toadflax from growing right up through a hummock of dropseed and continue on its way. Similarly, in the savannas Penn sedge seems to be a protector of many delicate spring forbs.

What we've also seen over time is that some of these aggressive matrix plants themselves start to break down in a healthy ecosystem. Where in the first ten years you may have a dense patch of, say, *Carex trichocarpa*, it starts to break down. At the start, it is very aggressive because it is roaming through the wet soils, basically with no competition. But all of a sudden, it just starts to break down. It's still there, but in amongst it is starting to show up...everything. So even if we get some of these warrior sedges too dense in the beginning, we believe they will also allow all the forbs to come in, and yet still control the area against weeds.

I should add that this is what we're finding in the Barrington area with our soil types and conditions. It's very possible that these ten warriors would be slightly different for ecosystems that are sand-dominated, floodplain, mesic, and so forth.

FIVE MOST WANTED
Sedge Meadow Invaders

With a history of taking over wetlands, these fast growers belong at the top of your removal list. A few tips from Tom on handling them.

Reed Canary Grass

Reed canary seeds will blanket an area and find holes in your turf. A little patch of ground might have 15 little plants, but herbicide is only going to kill what it hits. Even the best applicator can't find them all, so you need to just keep following it up. Because of labeling, you'll need to wait to herbicide until standing water has dried up.

Phragmites
(aka Common Reed)

It's hard to spot an individual spike of phragmites, but you can do it if you know what they look like. It's so much easier to kill a few spikes than getting a 15-foot patch. In large areas, it will have killed most native vegetation, so you can use a general herbicide. For smaller patches, use grass-selective herbicide.

Purple Loosestrife

If you kill one loosestrife before it blooms, it doesn't get to set its thousands of seeds. We want to kill one loosestrife, not 25 in two years because we didn't get this one. We usually hand wick loosestrife.

Cattail

The wetter the soil, the more cattail seedlings come. As light germinators, they readily germinate in bare soils. When a beaver dam breaks and leaves exposed mud, it's all cattails within a year. Pull cattail seedlings in their first month. Otherwise, they will have sent out rhizomes and you'll have to hand wick them.

Scirpus

The native river bulrush, *Scirpus fluviatilis*, can be very aggressive and take over wetlands. Little else can grow with it, so make sure to keep an eye on this often-overlooked invasive.

Top of Mind

Tom recommends keeping these things top of mind as you restore sedge meadow (and other habitats).

1. Save remnants at all costs.

Any pocket of sedge meadow from before European settlement is irreplaceable and invaluable. Take time to understand what's there, and protect every part you can. Herbicide-susceptible native grasses can be protected under buckets, if necessary.

2. Find a way.

Restoration will always throw you little curveballs. Be observant and creative enough to get around it and not create a roadblock. Think: what *can* we do?

3. Go back, go back, go back.

Just because you think you've removed all invasives doesn't mean they're gone. Be extremely vigilant in following up with spot herbicide across your entire site. "Go back" many times in seeding, too, since some years' seed may not be very viable.

4. Rally volunteers with mileposts.

The scope of even a small restoration can be daunting, but don't forget that as soon as the land begins to recover, nature will throw volunteers all kinds of encouraging signs and learning opportunities.

5. Follow the entire sequence.

Skipping steps in the sequence or thinking you've succeeded after the first few may leave you back at square one. Follow-through is essential.

6. Keep eyes on the ground.

Nothing can replace volunteers walking the site on a regular basis, looking for new invaders as well as successes. This could be a formal monitoring program or just a posse of volunteers who like to take regular walks.

7. Read the landscape and be flexible.

Conditions on the ground are always changing — new invasives, fluctuating water levels, unexpected weather. A steward has to constantly read these changes and be ready to adapt.

3 Sedge Meadow Mistakes

Drought
Sedge plugs will fail if they're not kept saturated. Make sure to water them for the first year if they're in a dry location.

Resources not ready
Stay organized, with a mix of resources ready to deploy. Whether it be volunteers, interns, or contractors, be ready to do what needs to be done when conditions are right.

Quitting too soon
This can't be said enough. You can't work hard for two years, then just let it go. (Many contracts work on this timeframe.) Think five years, or ten.

Return on Investment

What's coming back to Flint Creek Savanna's restored sedge meadow?

By 2017, the ten warrior sedges had formed a matrix along Flint Creek and were joined by other native plants. What were once dwindling, disconnected remnants began to feel more like contiguous stretches of habitat that wildlife would actually use.

"You're getting this positive feedback," says Tom. "Because while the restoration is going on, great amounts of native plants are surging forward, things are getting better and better, you're getting more and more psyched up. You know it's working. You have a bigger and bigger incentive to go get that remaining reed canary. Within two or three years, the birds are flying back in."

On a snowy December day in 2016, a pair of sandhill cranes were spotted picking through the meadow. "The sedge meadow is so diverse that, at this time of the year, they're probably not even getting frogs or crayfish," says Tom. "They're probably below surface by now. They're getting the tubers of the arrowheads and maybe other roots of different plants. And those are plants we've restored."

In 2011, near where sedge plugs had gone in, volunteers began seeing the remnant-dependent bronze copper butterfly. "Boom—right in there!" Tom says. "Here are our rare butterflies. They were in the remnant, but they weren't here."

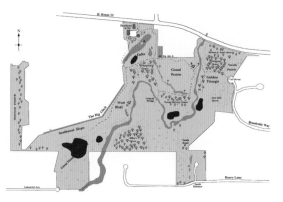

2000. Shortly after the purchase of Flint Creek Savanna, isolated sedge meadow remnants clung to life in a sea of reed canary grass.

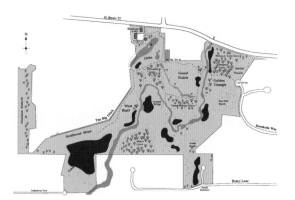

2017. CFC is halfway to its goal of healthy sedge meadow stretching continuously from one end of the 146-acre property to the other.

"The insects will come to the restorations if they can get there," says Tom. "Mammals, maybe. And some of this stuff we're going to have to bring in. But that's the fun of restoring whole sedge meadows."

Comeback Kids

These species returned, on their own, to about eight acres of restored sedge meadow along Flint Creek in Barrington. An anecdotal list, as reported by CFC volunteers.

1. Bronze copper butterfly

2. Black dash skipper

3. Dion skipper

4. Big-eyed brown

5. Sandhill crane

6. Swamp sparrow

7. Sedge wren

8. Marsh wren

9. Bur reed moth

10. Muskrat

11. Mink

12. Green frog

13. Leopard frog

14. Black-legged katydid

15. Water heartsease

The Future

Plans, Experiments, Technology

Artificial Hummocks

CFC has been making artificial sedge hummocks for years, but now they're experimenting with entire prefab plant communities. These hummocks will comingle sedges and forbs grown from seed. See facing page for how they plan to do it.

Tiptoeing Tank

To improve efficiency in herbiciding larger areas, CFC just started using a Marsh Master. The vehicle's treads spread pressure across the ground to prevent soil compaction and plant damage.

Foxholes for Turtles

Based on research from McHenry County, Tom hopes to support Blanding's turtle reproduction by adding hatchling-sized holes in CFC's artificial hummocks where young turtles can hide from predators.

How to Make a Hummock

Making artificial sedge hummocks takes a few years, but it just might give your restoration a big boost in stability and diversity. CFC believes this new technique could be an ideal way to establish hard-to-seed conservative species.

1. Collect seed.

The season before you make hummocks, collect seed and stratify over winter. Focus on a few dozen rare and delicate species such as marsh harebell, marsh bedstraw, marsh cinquefoil, cardinal flower, great blue lobelia, even showy lady slipper and white fringed orchid if regulations allow.

2. Get your pot.

Fiber pots can be purchased online or at hardware stores and garden shops. Get the three-gallon ones that are guaranteed to last for at least three years — otherwise, they'll disintegrate too soon. Fill the pot with soil.

3. Plant sedge.

Plant one sedge plug in the first year. Use Carex stricta. Since it doesn't aggressively send out rhizomes, this species often falls over as a lonely plug and benefits greatly from the support of a hummock.

4. Use a holding bed.

If you have the space and resources, you can make an outdoor wetland nursery to ensure that your hummock is always moist. (Otherwise, just be sure to water vigilantly.)

5. Sow seed.

Seed in your conservatives around the sedge. Some will germinate in the first year, others won't. If, by year two, you don't have 20 to 30 plants germinating, sow again.

6. Install in restoration.

Plant your hummock during step 4 of the Sedge Meadow Sequence (p. 50). Established upon a C. stricta hummock, your rare orchids and associates will have a much better chance of survival.

Notes

About Tom Vanderpoel

A landscaper by trade, Tom Vanderpoel joined Citizens for Conservation (CFC) in 1984. He sat on CFC's board, serving as restoration committee chair and restoration director, as well as on its land acquisition team. Since 1986, he led the group's pioneering habitat restoration efforts, establishing some of the finest restorations in the Chicago region and constantly striving for more effective techniques. Tom's applied knowledge and understanding were matched by an exceptional generosity of spirit. He always had time for a restoration question, confident that it would take a community, and generations, to complete the work. He consulted on restoration projects for the Forest Preserves of Cook County, The Nature Conservancy, and Audubon – Chicago Region. As we finalized text and amassed the art for this chapter, we suddenly lost Tom. His generous teaching nurtured a community of committed and knowledgeable restorationists – arguably his greatest achievement. This dedicated community will carry his work forward.

About Citizens for Conservation

Founded in 1971, Citizens for Conservation (CFC) is a nonprofit volunteer organization dedicated to preserving native habitat in and around Barrington, Illinois. The group led the Barrington Greenway Initiative to protect more than 3,100 local acres, and catalyzed the creation of four new forest preserves. CFC also protects 476 acres over 11 of its own properties. Having established itself as an innovator in restoration techniques (such as its famous floating islands), CFC holds regular restoration workdays, runs an intern program, and contracts with outside restoration companies. CFC holds regular education programs for the public and promotes environmental practices that enhance ecosystem services. To volunteer or learn more, visit citizensforconservation.org.

POINT OF CRAFT

A Twist on Brushpile Building

WITH CLIFFORD SCHULTZ

For CFC volunteer Cliff Schultz, a retired middle-school math teacher and avowed problem solver, burning brushpiles is an art and science. Some groups toss on brush every which way, which can result in a sloppy pile with a big footprint. Cliff's technique, which works best when burning solo or with small groups, relies on a "brushpile czar" regulating what goes in when, building a brushpile that's compact and fast-burning.

Keep the pile under 6 feet across and 6 feet tall.

With the fire well established, feather longer, larger branches into gaps and through the middle of the fire to maintain core temps.

Add heavier logs to crush down twigs.

Layer on thicker branches, around 1.5 inch diameter, "like railroad tracks."

START with a bed of dead twigs, up to .5 inch in diameter. Try to keep branches parallel as you layer higher and higher. Ignite deadwood.

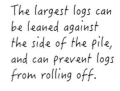

The largest logs can be leaned against the side of the pile, and can prevent logs from rolling off.

Add a layer of spindly branches to space out the pile. "It's an Oreo cookie strategy," says Cliff. "Alternating layers allows you to build compactly, but with air pockets."

As the fire builds heat, cut smaller-diameter top branches off green buckthorn and build a layer on top, up to 12 inches thick. Rotate each new layer 30° to 45° from previous one.

Monitoring
Fit for a Steward

with Dr. Karen Glennemeier

Is your restoration working? Inside some volunteer-scaled techniques to assess your effectiveness and adapt management.

Karen Glennemeier is a monitoring midwife of sorts.

Between 2002 and 2005, Karen, then with Audubon – Chicago Region, organized the mobilization of some 200 citizen scientists for the Chicago Wilderness Woods Audit and its successor, the Grassland Audit. Training volunteers to locate random coordinates, navigate obstacles, and set up survey plots, she paired experts with novices and dispatched teams to get familiar with patches of ground most of us would never even think to visit. In all, volunteers recorded data for 322 plots or transects across 198,000 acres of protected public natural land in 8 counties. The effort resulted in the most comprehensive picture of the ecological health of our region's natural areas before or since.

Through Audubon's Habitat Project, Karen supported monitors of all stripes – birds, butterflies, dragonflies, frogs, and other groups – connecting them with stewards and land managers to better inform management activities.

In the course of her work, Karen has counseled scores of stewards in monitoring the preserves under their care. Most haunt their sites like restless spirits and know them extremely well. True to the old proverb – "the best fertilizer is the gardener's shadow" – they've been over every square inch hundreds of times, spending years and even decades restoring and watching the land change.

Still, Karen says, stewards approach her wanting to know whether they should put more effort into quantifying their restoration work, seeking ways they can practically add monitoring to an already full job. They ask everything from how to design a transect to how to build a quadrat. (Hint: It's really, really easy.)

Even among highly observant stewards, how well do we really know our sites? Do we fully understand how things have changed? How accurate is our recollection of past conditions? Could we convincingly demonstrate the impact our restoration actions are having? Is our site

Inspecting a quadrat for the Grassland Audit in 2005.

healthy? Is it getting better? Are we actively consulting data to direct our next actions?

And beyond that, what can we say about how the land functions? Do we know even the majority of species that use it as habitat? Do we know who visits, when they come and go, and how they use the landscape? What about nutrient cycling, air and water quality, carbon capture? These are just some of the potentially transformative questions that monitoring can begin to answer.

Depending on what you want to know, scientific monitoring can get pretty time-intensive, technical, and challenging. A person could spend years and get a PhD learning how to research the land.

But there are also plenty of ways to keep it simple, get lots of useful information, and leave time for core restoration work. As a starting point, this chapter focuses mainly on plants, boiling monitoring down to its essentials and an à la carte menu of techniques. Even a very modest, focused monitoring effort can greatly improve outcomes, understanding, and satisfaction, says Karen. "It's more intuitive than you might think," she says, "more common sense than anything. And maybe that's helpful. You know, you really can do this."

5 Reasons to Start Monitoring

Why monitor? Karen makes the case for giving it a try.

1. Practice adaptive management.

For many stewards, informing adaptive management is the main reason to monitor, the principal means to understand what's working and what's not, so you can adjust your restoration practices. Are you actually meeting your management goals?

2. Master time.

Track your site through time and capture its history. Understand trends. Remember where you've been and what you've done.

3. Tell a better story.

"Another important reason could be to demonstrate the value of your restoration project," says Karen, "or to demonstrate to a funder, a boss, or a community that this place is actually getting healthier." Arm yourself with facts and figures to tell a better story about the benefits a site is providing to volunteers and the community at large.

4. Keep yourself honest.

"Monitoring keeps you honest," says Karen. "It's so easy to just glaze over the details, either because it's hard to see them or you've got a kind of preconceived notion of what it should be. And when you take data, it just forces you to see, 'Oh, this is better than I thought, or this is worse than I thought.'"

5. See differently.

Monitoring forces you to go places you wouldn't otherwise go, to discover species, places, and site features you didn't know you had. "I thought I was setting up a bunch of salamander boards in areas of super-dense tall goldenrod," says Karen, "and then I went out there this week to actually collect data. And it's just amazing; you get down in there you're like, 'Wow, there's a lot of goldenrod here, but there's all this other great stuff in among it.' Monitoring provides the opportunity to follow your curiosity in a more thorough way, finally answer your burning questions, and have fun in the process.

Too Late To Begin?

What if you've already been restoring a site for ten years? Is it too late to get a baseline? "As with anything, of course it's never too late," says Karen. "Start now. You will wish you had started 10 years ago, but start now — you'll be glad you did. There's always stuff to learn because the ecosystem's always changing."

"If your site is big," she says, "and there are places that you haven't yet started restoring, take data there now, because it will be really fun to see those numbers change over time."

Inside Mindful Monitoring

Monitoring is more than transects and quadrats. It's an intentional process of thinking and questioning to help us notice changes on the ground.

❶ Walk Your Site

You're probably doing it already, but nothing is more important than being out on the ground, again and again. It's probably the most powerful habit of successful stewardship.

❷ Add a Notebook

Get yourself a nice one. (See page 72).

❸ Write Down Everything

Capture observations, species lists, maps, and sketches of important features. Most importantly, write down your questions. What do you want to learn?

❹ Boil It Down

Over time, the many questions often coalesce to a critical few — usually the ones you find yourself asking over and over.

❺ Find Your Method

Let your questions lead to an appropriate monitoring method. Some stewards may find that journaling is all they need. Others will want to go deeper into quantification, or measure something specific later on. Check with the landowner to see if they have a preferred protocol.

❻ Get Monitoring!

Start small. Make sure it's something you can finish.

❼ Call For Backup

If something is beyond your expertise or you don't have time for monitoring, ask others for help. There may be plant, bird, frog, snake, insect, or whatever-else monitors who would love to take on your site. Looking through more than one lens (not just plants) will help you understand your site more fully. More eyes also increase objectivity — and the number of people falling in love with a place.

❽ Change Management (Or Not)

Unless you're just monitoring for curiosity, be ready to make changes in how you're restoring. It can feel oddly like a leap of faith, but responding to your results is what adaptive management is all about.

❾ Revisit Your Questions

Learning about your site may change what you want to know going forward. You can adjust your monitoring focus over time to best serve your needs, though don't lightly abandon worthwhile long-term investigations.

❿ Revisit Notes

Periodically re-read your notes. It'll remind you what you've done, how a site has changed, and suggest paths forward — including more monitoring.

⓫ Share Your Work

Share your data and the story they tell with other stewards, volunteers, ecologists, and people outside the choir, too. (See page 89.)

Write It Down!

If you do one thing to know your site better, visit it more often. If you do two things, start writing. It's the gateway to good monitoring.

Writing is a critical part of the process of looking and thinking that habitat restoration requires – but not everyone does it.

"If you do nothing else, write it down," says Karen. "Write down what you're seeing and what you're thinking. It'll add up to more than you realize."

"Just doing that is already a kind of qualitative monitoring, in the sense of 'Oh, the purple loosestrife looks terrible' this year, it's up to the edge of such and such. I'm trying this.' And then you try it and you go back next year and write, 'It still looks really bad.' And then the next year, 'Hey, I think it looks better.' And over seven years, you've got a trend. You've written it down. 'Ohhh, that's *riiiight*! Back seven years ago it was all the way out to here, and now it's here. It *is* getting better.'"

Writing things down helps guard against repeating mistakes. "One thing that I do all the time in my yard is I have a garden journal," Karen says. "And if I didn't have that journal, I would keep doing the same failed things every year – literally, because I always think I'm gonna remember, and then winter happens and my brain gets erased, and I look at my notes and I think, 'Gah, I have no memory of having done that!' And it's the reason that I can raise tomatoes from seeds successfully now, because every year I write down, 'Well I tried this and that didn't work. Next year, try this.' And next year I try it. And so it's scientific in a sort of trial-and-error, iterative way. It's not like I set up experiments to test different techniques, but.... I think writing things down is – I don't know if it's universal, but for me it's the difference between night and day.

"So, I think that could be a huge step for a great many stewards, to just write stuff down, and describe it in a way that, when they go back and look at it ten years later, they'll know what that was telling them."

"I'm a big fan of drawings," says Karen. "For visual people at least, sketches help jog memory better than words." Unlined or dotted paper is good for sketches, maps, and graphs.

"One of my favorite things," she says, "is to look back over notes that help me remember the exact day I was out there, the people I was with when I learned a new plant, or other tidbits that feel more like a personal journal than just a scientific set of observations."

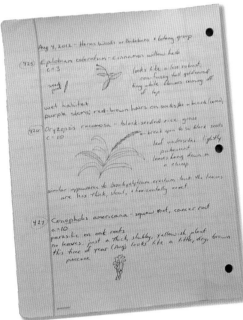

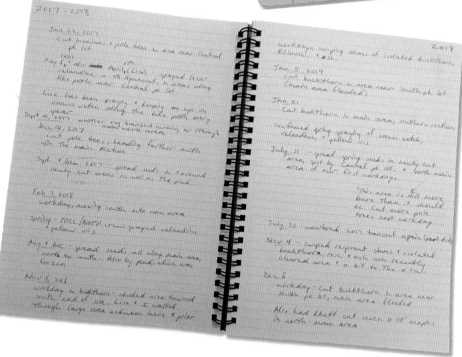

Facing page: Karen recommends getting a notebook that sings to you and fits just right in your pocket or backpack. "I love mine," she says. "When I pick it up, it makes me happy."

Go as digital as you like. Karen has scanned all her plant sketches into a tablet to create a searchable database for plant ID. "Searchability comes in really handy once you've built up many years of notes," she says.

A Continuum of Observation

Monitoring isn't monolithic. It includes a range of valuable techniques, which you can choose based on your needs and resources.

Wandering Inventory

Keep a running list of the species you encounter on walks through your site. This method won't tell you much about trends, but it will give you a cumulative picture of what's there, often capturing more total species than other methods. It can be used for plants, wildlife, or anything else.

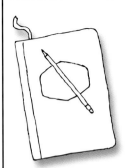

Journal

Write down things you notice, questions you have, things you want to remember. Keep it all together in one place.

Focus Areas

Keep things manageable by narrowing your focus to a specific question or geographic area.

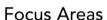

Increasing complexity, time, and effort

Increasing data yield, objectivity, quantification

Rapid Assessment

These shortcut surveys can give you a broadstroke picture of your entire site and reveal useful trends. Some are shorter than others. See page 80.

Transect

Transects can be done on their own or as part of a larger survey. They go from "transect lite" (e.g., lay out just one transect and only record the presence or absence of invasives) all the way to a supersized version (e.g., multiple transects with many points, recording all species and multiple plot characteristics, etc.). See page 78.

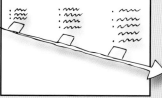

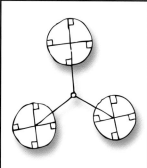

Full Species Assessment

This is an intensive survey giving you the fullest picture of your site. A lot of work goes into survey design and execution, usually as part of a larger study. See page 82.

Know Your Why

BY KAREN GLENNEMEIER

The most important thing people need to do in monitoring – the first step – is to ask, *What do I want to know? What is my question? What do I want to learn?*

Maybe your question is *I want to know the floristic quality of my site and how that's changing over time*. The gold standard for measuring that is to lay out transects, put down a quadrat, record all the species and their percent cover. Then you pretty much know everything there is to know about the vegetation community, and you can go back later and ask different questions. But that's a lot of work, a lot of knowledge, and a lot of inertia to be overcome. Most people don't do it.

But maybe your most pressing question, practically, is, *Is tall goldenrod decreasing?* That's a much simpler thing to monitor. In that case, you can say, I just want to know if tall goldenrod's going down; so I'm going to go out with my quadrat frame, along a transect, through just that area, and I'm going to plop it down every 10 steps, and I'm going to look at tall goldenrod and say "20 percent." Then I'm going to do it, here and I'm gonna say "40 percent." And it's going to take me 20 minutes instead of three hours. Just getting really clear about *Why do I think I need to monitor, what is it that I wish I knew?* That helps focus you: *Okay, what do I need to do to get the answer?*

But how do you even figure out what you want to know? Pay attention to what you're thinking about when you're out there. Stewards are constantly asking themselves questions – I know I am. You do your workday and you come back later and you're like, "Oooh, I wonder this." So notice what you're thinking and write it down.

Start writing, and you'll start to realize what you need to be monitoring. *I want there to be a higher diversity of plants*. Oh, well I guess I should be measuring that, to see if I'm actually achieving that. *I want to bring more light in*. Oh, okay, I can measure that. I can just go out and stand, and instead of looking down, I'm gonna look up. Or I could go out on a sunny day and look down and just look at the shade. To be more objective, I might use a light meter.

But there's more. Underneath *What do I want to know?* lie still more fundamental questions: *What am I trying to do? What's the goal of our stewardship? Why are we out there?* If, for instance, you don't care about Floristic Quality Index, and the goal of your stewardship is to decrease streambank erosion, then you would want to focus your monitoring on exposed roots or other direct measures of erosion. So the first question is really, *Why are we managing? What's our goal?* Taking the time to think through these questions carefully will give your restoration work a much more solid foundation.

The Essence of Monitoring

Most ecological monitoring boils down to a single concept with endless variations and applications.

Basic Building Block: The Transect

"Walk a regular route that represents the area and stop at a predetermined interval to measure the thing you're interested in," says Karen. (This is "walking a transect.")

With adjustments, she says, this can be applied to everything from plants to birds. "What data you take and in what configuration is infinitely variable."

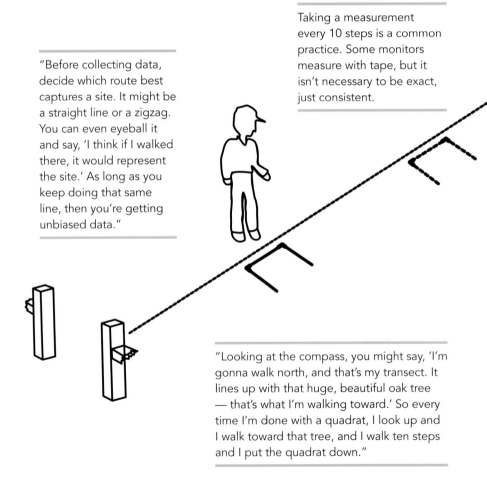

Taking a measurement every 10 steps is a common practice. Some monitors measure with tape, but it isn't necessary to be exact, just consistent.

"Before collecting data, decide which route best captures a site. It might be a straight line or a zigzag. You can even eyeball it and say, 'I think if I walked there, it would represent the site.' As long as you keep doing that same line, then you're getting unbiased data."

"Looking at the compass, you might say, 'I'm gonna walk north, and that's my transect. It lines up with that huge, beautiful oak tree — that's what I'm walking toward.' So every time I'm done with a quadrat, I look up and I walk toward that tree, and I walk ten steps and I put the quadrat down."

Avoid Bias

"If you want an objective picture, you have to walk a path based on something other than what you're measuring, such as a compass point, tree in the distance, whatever. Otherwise, you may end up measuring the stuff that you really like, or that is easy to measure, or something else that biases your answer."

Good communication with the landowner can facilitate coordination with existing monitoring efforts. A permit also may be required for certain types of monitoring.

"If it's one species you're interested in, that's all you have to look for. If it's everything, then you need to know all your plants. If you just want to know grasses versus forbs versus invasives versus bare ground — that tells you a lot, too."

Aim to record 10 to 20 points in your area of interest — enough to gather good data but still something you're likely to repeat.

How Often Should I Monitor? And For How Long?

"It depends," says Karen. "Ask yourself over what timeframe you expect to see change. If I know it's going to take three years to see species coming up from seeds I spread, I'm gonna do it every three years.

"Or it may be easier to try to do it once a year. But you might have to base your timing on the activity of your subject, such as woodland ephemerals in April and May.

"And it's okay if you miss a year," she says. "Keep doing it!"

Rapid Assessments, 3 Ways

Local organizations have had success with new methods for quickly judging the integrity of plant communities. While some approach formal monitoring, they're all more attainable for busy volunteers than full assessments.

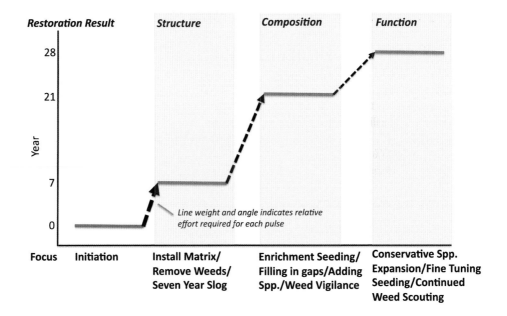

Qualitative Rapid Assessment

A method being developed by the Barrington Greenway Initiative, a multi-partner effort spearheaded by Citizens for Conservation, is aimed at improving stewards' ability to assess a site at a glance. The technique breaks the restoration process into three phases. Stewards look for certain characteristics to determine where a site falls. For the first two phases, stewards mainly need to know the worst invasive weeds (aka "barrier species") such as buckthorn and reed canary grass and a relatively short list of native matrix species for each habitat, such as prairie dropseed and little bluestem.

- Phase 1: Structure (getting the right shape)
  You're ridding the site of the barrier invasives to return to a structure more like a healthy ecosystem.

- Phase 2: Composition (getting the right species)
  Barrier species are gone. Native matrix species dominate, with an ever more diverse plant community. By the end, even minor weeds are few and far between.

- Phase 3: Function (getting the final parts in place)
  You've reached this fine-tuning phase when your site supports many of the most conservative plants and can be maintained entirely by fire.

Plant Functional Group Density

Since 2017, the Forest Preserves of Cook County has been piloting the Mean Plant Functional Group Density method, a rapid assessment developed by researchers Valerie Sivicek and John Taft. Instead of recording every plant species, monitors rate habitats by the presence of functional groups, such as sedges, cool-season grasses, warm-season grasses, perennial forbs, and others. Many of these groups can be broadly identified based on physical characteristics, although monitors still need a good grasp on plant ID. "It seems to track well with other indicators of vegetation quality," says Rebecca Collings, senior resource ecologist at the Forest Preserve District of Cook County (FPCC), although she says it may not detect small changes in quality over time.

- Takes roughly 25% less time than full species assessment, depending on the quality of the site and knowledge of the monitor.

- Used at more than 10 volunteer stewardship sites.

Rapid Floristic Quality Assessment

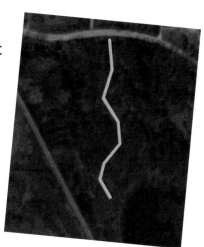

For the Centennial Volunteers initiative, Friends of the Chicago River borrowed a Rapid Floristic Quality Assessment (FQA) method from the Minnesota Pollution Control Agency to assess 15 restoration sites across the Chicago area. "Using this method, we found that native plant coverage increased from 46% to 70% since 2016," says Friends ecology outreach manager Mark Hauser. "It's a testament to the thousands of volunteers who have put in long hours and dedicated themselves to transforming these river-edge preserves."

- The monitor performs one timed meandering transect for each site — no fixed points or equipment needed.

- Monitor can cover about 10 feet per minute, or 600 feet every hour.

- Can be used to calculate mean and weighted coefficient of conservatism, floristic quality index (FQI), and percent native coverage.

To learn more, visit pca.state.mn.us/water/floristic-quality-assessment-evaluating-wetland-vegetation

The Full Monty

Want to do a full plant species assessment? A peek at one method.

You can inform your management using a less intensive method, but if you have the time and energy, a full plant species assessment can yield a trove of useful data. There are many ways to do it, but here's a look at the design Karen used for the 2008 Cook County Land Audit, which is based on a protocol by John Taft of the Illinois Natural History Survey.

1. Generate random points.

Scientists often use computer programs to do this, but other methods work, too. (Darts, anyone?) The Land Audit randomly selected points within 15,000 acres of Cook County forest preserve previously identified as fair quality or better.

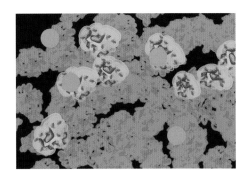

Universal Protocol?
Use 1/4 m² Quadrat

Having a common standard for collecting data allows ecologists to share data, compare trends, and study larger phenomena across jurisdictions.

Over the years, Chicago-region agencies have worked to align protocols. "The problem is that everybody's got their own thing," says Karen.

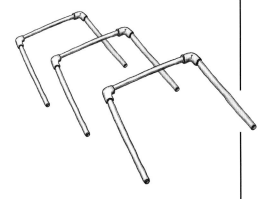

What's a collaboratively minded steward to do? "The thing that matters most if you want to be able to compare your data to others' is your sample unit size," says Karen. "Which is why we've at least settled on using the 1/4 m² quadrat, a square with half-meter-long sides. You can do a lot if you're using the same base unit size."

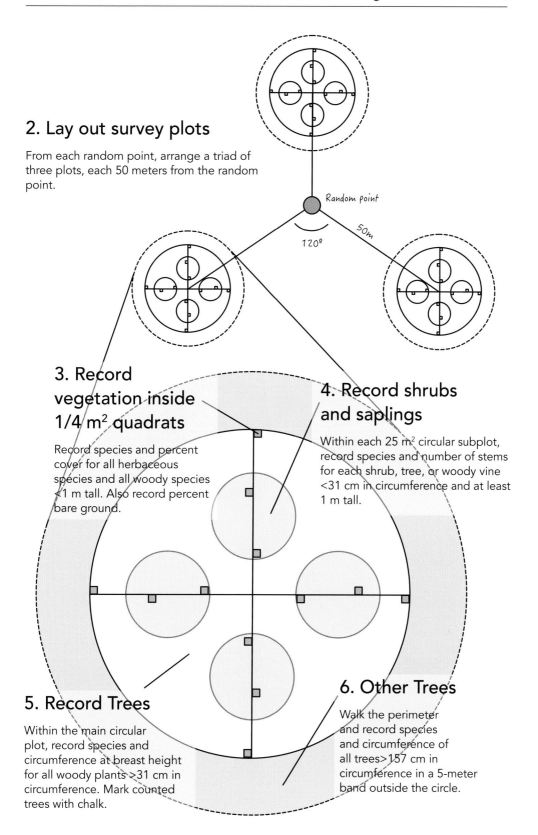

2. Lay out survey plots

From each random point, arrange a triad of three plots, each 50 meters from the random point.

Random point

120º

50m

3. Record vegetation inside 1/4 m² quadrats

Record species and percent cover for all herbaceous species and all woody species <1 m tall. Also record percent bare ground.

4. Record shrubs and saplings

Within each 25 m² circular subplot, record species and number of stems for each shrub, tree, or woody vine <31 cm in circumference and at least 1 m tall.

5. Record Trees

Within the main circular plot, record species and circumference at breast height for all woody plants >31 cm in circumference. Mark counted trees with chalk.

6. Other Trees

Walk the perimeter and record species and circumference of all trees>157 cm in circumference in a 5-meter band outside the circle.

Tools to Tally

Although some kinds of monitoring require specialized equipment, the requirements for plant monitoring are minimal.

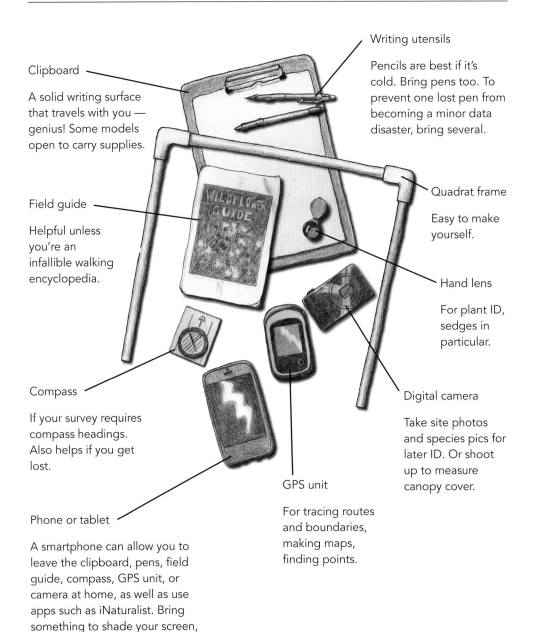

Writing utensils

Pencils are best if it's cold. Bring pens too. To prevent one lost pen from becoming a minor data disaster, bring several.

Clipboard

A solid writing surface that travels with you — genius! Some models open to carry supplies.

Quadrat frame

Easy to make yourself.

Field guide

Helpful unless you're an infallible walking encyclopedia.

Hand lens

For plant ID, sedges in particular.

Compass

If your survey requires compass headings. Also helps if you get lost.

Digital camera

Take site photos and species pics for later ID. Or shoot up to measure canopy cover.

GPS unit

For tracing routes and boundaries, making maps, finding points.

Phone or tablet

A smartphone can allow you to leave the clipboard, pens, field guide, compass, GPS unit, or camera at home, as well as use apps such as iNaturalist. Bring something to shade your screen, as bright prairie sunlight can make it harder to see.

How to
Make a Quadrat Frame

It's almost too easy to make your own quadrat frame. The key is to build the right size: quarter-meter-squared — big enough to capture diversity, but not so big as to make estimating things like percent cover exhausting. This is also the standard for most botanists, so it'll be easier to compare results with others.

1. Get the parts!

At your local hardware store, purchase:

• 3 half-meter lengths of PVC pipe, half-inch diameter. (Many stores will cut lengths for you.)

• 2 half-inch-diameter PVC elbow joints

2. Put them together!

The parts should fit snugly together. (One side of the square is purposely left open.) Leaving the parts unglued will allow you to disassemble them for storage, if desired.

Surveying Shortcuts

Depending on what you're trying to learn, one of these techniques might save you time and get you where you want to go.

Shrink the Universe

Your "sample universe" is the scope of things you focus on. Save time by narrowing that focus. "Say I'm just interested in this one little corner," says Karen. "I don't think it represents the site, but this is a corner I care about. Then I can just monitor that corner. It depends on my question."

Presence/Absence

"Instead of measuring the abundance of something within a quadrat, you can just measure presence/absence, says Karen. "Is tall goldenrod in my quadrat or not? Over twenty plots, you're actually getting that abundance data. It's a coarser resolution, but it's much easier, much faster, and it might be enough for a lot of purposes."

Creative Measurement

No equipment? You can take measurements just using your body or things around the house. "It's nice to have something like a quadrat," says Karen, "but you can also use something like a hula hoop, especially if you're just measuring presence/absence."

"Another thing people do, more for things like shrubs where there are fewer of them, is just walk a line and say, 'If it falls within my outstretched arms, I'm going to count that stem.' So that could be something you use for measuring woody invasives."

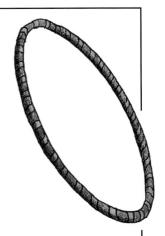

Seed Circles

If you're raking leaf litter to expose the soil when seeding, this can be a great opportunity for focused monitoring.

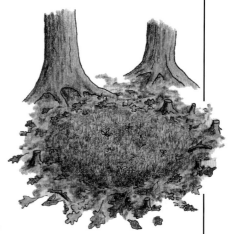

"You've spread seeds in a circle this big because you had to rake that circle," says Karen. "You can seed that circle for many years, and you can go back every year to see if it changes over time. You'll know the 20 species you spread, so you can just look for those. It becomes a natural monitoring unit."

Karen says watching the areas where you've put precious seed will help you determine the success of each species and whether to keep seeding it there: "Okay, we spread those gentian seeds, and ten years later, they're not coming up. So we need to stop wasting gentian seed until we figure out what's going on."

The Sedge Hedge

Keying out sedges takes time to master, but don't let that hold you back. "The vast majority of local sedges are species we want," says Karen. "It's not like half of them are terrible. So if you know it's a sedge, but not which sedge, and you need to assign a C-value for your calculations, 3 is a pretty safe average for most of our common sedge species."

Apps & Other E-Helpers

iNaturalist
Record, map, and share plant discoveries, plus get real-time ID help from real people. This app is "pretty remarkable," says Karen.

GPS Apps
"For the technically inclined, you can see the line you walked and overlay it with management." Karen uses GPS Tracks.

ArcGIS
A "super-simple subset of the big, fancy ArcGIS" mapping program, this free online version "does the basics, and it's not mind-boggling like the full thing."

Got Data — Now What?

Crunch the numbers. Answer your questions.

Unless you're planning to publish your results (which is a whole other conversation), that data you've collected was made to serve you. So first, put it in a form that's easy for you to work with and understand. Then put it to work answering your questions.

My	awesome	data
3.1	4.2	8.5
8.3	1.4	3.3
3.1	4.2	4.2
3.2	4.5	3.1

Enter It

Karen recommends entering all your data into a spreadsheet (on Excel or a similar program) "because then you can do math, organize, store, and share it, and find the data in the future." Or you can enter them into UniversalFQA.org (see next page). A monitoring protocol may also provide a data sheet.

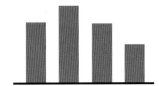

Graph It

"If you want to see things changing over time, make a graph," says Karen. Most spreadsheet applications (e.g., Excel, Numbers, Google) have graphing functions built right in.

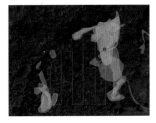

Map It

"It can be super helpful to look at a map and say, 'Here's my monitoring route, and it's really high-quality here, and it's really low-quality here, and I'm gonna overlay our management.' And then you can physically see, 'We did this here and we didn't do this here, and it's correlating.'" Phone-based GPS apps make mapmaking easier than it used to be.

Do What Works For You

As with exercise, the best kind of monitoring is the kind you actually do. "If you really have no idea what you're doing, and you think you're bad at math, you can keep it very simple," says Karen. "Say you took ten quadrats, and you have the percent cover of tall goldenrod in each. Now take an average. You just want to know if the average is going up or down. And that's the number you're working with."

For a more rigorous approach, you can apply statistical techniques such as standard deviation and a standard error of the mean. (Karen can show you how.) "Statistics allow us to tell if the changes we're seeing over time or between two sites are 'real' versus just random bouncing up and down," says Karen. But simply collecting data and starting to make basic calculations can get you a long way.

Sharing Is Caring

Don't lock those insights away in a dusty cabinet.

Why proactively share your data and findings? "We all want to learn from your hard work!" says Karen. "You're not only informing your own management, but you're helping the rest of us adapt and improve as well. Conversely, other stewards and monitors and scientists may have insights into your data that you hadn't thought of."

Stewards group
Tell other stewards what you found and ask for their ideas.

Online platforms
ArcGIS and iNaturalist allow users to share a variety of data. Homegrown FQA calculator UniversalFQA.org connects you to the surveys of other local ecologists.

Journals
If your data point to something new and your methods are rigorous, publishing in a scientific journal is a way to share with a widespread, serious audience.

Landowner
Bring data to your partnership with agency staff and ecologists.

Friends, neighbors, partners
Don't assume ecologists are the only ones who might be interested. Share your exciting discoveries with everyone you meet. You never know who'll want to join in the botanizing.

Notes

About Karen Glennemeier

Kansas native Karen Glennemeier grew up playing on her grandparents' farm and traveling to national parks. Earning degrees in biology and endocrinology, including a PhD from the University of Michigan, she studied, among other things, the effects of environmental pollutants on the hormones and ecology of frogs.

In 2001, Karen joined Audubon – Chicago Region, where she would spend the next 13 years as science director. There, she conducted research and oversaw the Habitat Project, a network of more than 1,000 citizen scientists working together to answer the pressing questions of local habitat restoration.

In 2015, as an ecologist with Shedd Aquarium, Karen launched a volunteer-fueled restoration project to restore ephemeral ponds for amphibians at Bob Mann Woods in Westchester. It featured

a robust monitoring protocol to assess the work's effect on herps and plants, complete with plant quadrats and bucket sampling to count amphibian tadpoles.

In 2019, Karen started her own company, Habitat Research, where she consults on restoration, monitoring, and research efforts across the Chicago region.

Karen is also currently co-steward at Harms Woods East in Glenview and an advocate and advisor for urban habitat in her village of Wilmette. She spearheaded the creation of a six-acre native Lakefront Bird Habitat garden at Gillson Park near her family's home. Though Karen keeps busy with ecological stewardship and citizen activism, stroll down the street on a summer day and you may catch strains of her fiddle from the porch overlooking her frontyard prairie.

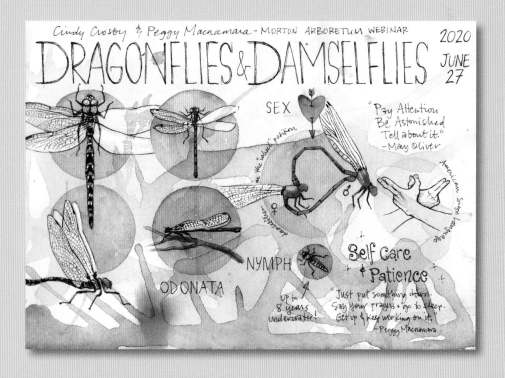

Monitor Birds, See Ecosystems in 3D

with Jenny Flexman

Better accounting for birds and other wildlife can give critical perspective on the ecological health of your site.

A northern harrier slices through the crisp air above the prairie. Coursing back and forth, it surveys. In an instant, it pauses and drops. Breakfast is served.

Harriers and other raptors —not to mention humans — rely on binocular vision to survive. Having eyes spaced widely apart provides two separate perspectives, giving these hunters excellent spatial awareness and allowing them to react with surgical precision when a meal presents itself. Harriers' hearing, unique among daytime raptors, adds yet another stream of feedback.

Stewards can similarly gain three-dimensional vision by adding new lenses as they consider their restorations.

The experience of Schaumburg Road Grasslands steward Jenny Flexman is a case in point. For the first few decades she was involved

in habitat restoration, Jenny volunteered with the Poplar Creek Prairie Stewards at Carl Hansen Woods and Shoe Factory Road Prairie near Schaumburg, Illinois. There she focused on building a botanical knowledge base, learning the plants that define high-quality ecosystems. She still cites that as one of her proudest accomplishments.

But in the late 2000s, birders were sounding the alarm at a 200-acre site just south of Poplar Creek. The former farm fields, known as Schaumburg Road Grasslands, were being overtaken by brush, and the grassland birds that relied on them were dwindling. Grassland birds are North America's most imperiled avian group. Migrating from as far away as Argentina, their survival depends on habitat conditions across the western hemisphere. The wise management of their breeding grounds – the old-field meadows, hayfields, pastures, and prairies (both remnant and

Monitoring opened the world of grassland birds to Jenny Flexman, informing stewardship at Schaumburg Road from day one.

restored) across the Midwest – is critical to their survival.

The Prairie Stewards decided to adopt Schaumburg Road, with Jenny becoming steward. That shift helped reawaken a passion from earlier in Jenny's life. "I was a birder when I was 16 years old," she says. "Then I got away from it." Although Jenny was less familiar with grassland birds, other birders mentored her. What she found over the next decade is that by looking at the specific needs of target species – adding the lens of wildlife monitoring – she was able to better understand the results of the restoration. The birds gave her binocular acuity on her life's work.

When stewards manage plant communities, we're pulling levers for animals, too–be it birds, mammals, herps, or insects. Most of us recognize that animals are present on a site, and that they use the habitat in various ways, but we don't have the full picture. Adding a "stretch goal" to more quantitatively account for trends in wildlife populations – even just one or two taxa –can help us think about complex impacts and interrelations more fully.

So how to amp up your understanding? It's often easier than you think. Jenny spends a total of just six to nine hours a year doing the field observations that have yielded so much insight. Here is a glimpse into her transformation from steward to bird-steward, and how she came to better comprehend and manage one dynamic Illinois grassland.

Bird Monitors Raise First Flags

Monitoring turned attention to Schaumburg Road Grasslands, opening the latest chapter of bird-focused stewardship.

Researchers study and learn

In the spring and summer of 1995 and 1996, Charles "Chip" O'Leary (now deputy director of resource management for the Forest Preserves of Cook County) and University of Illinois at Chicago associate professor Dennis Nyberg surveyed breeding grassland birds at Schaumburg Road Grasslands for Chip's graduate thesis, published as *Treelines Between Fields Reduce the Density of Grassland Birds* (*Natural Areas Journal*, 2000). The study showed the strong preference of obligate grassland birds to nest in open meadows at least 50 meters from woodland edges, and recommended hedgerow removal in managing for grassland birds. "That was my guiding light at the beginning," says Jenny. "I first looked at it because it was specifically about my site, but what was most helpful was what it had to say about the territories of grassland birds."

Birders sound the alarm

By the 2000s, birders had grown worried about Schaumburg Road. Between 1998 and 2002, Lee Ramsey, a volunteer leader with the Bird Conservation Network (BCN), found low numbers of obligate grassland birds in breeding surveys. Those that remained were confined mostly to the small remaining open portion of the site. When he returned a few years later, the hedgerows and invasive shrubs had expanded even more. Soon staff from Audubon – Chicago Region, the Forest Preserves of Cook County (FPCC), and Poplar Creek Prairie Stewards walked the fields, eventually adding Schaumburg Road as a volunteer stewardship site.

Setting Up the Route

In 1998, Lee Ramsey established a monitoring route to quantify bird populations across Schaumburg Road Grasslands' 120 open acres. He handed that route to Jenny in 2010, and she's been using it ever since. Here's how it works.

"We follow the Bird Conservation Network protocol," says Jenny. "Lee designed the route to try to cover as much of the grassland as posssible. So we had 10 point counts within what we ended up making as grasslands." The three easternmost points are in shrubland.

Take care not to count the same bird twice.

Start as soon after sunrise as possible, and wrap up before 9 am. (After 9, summer birds are far less active.)

Points are 150 meters apart.

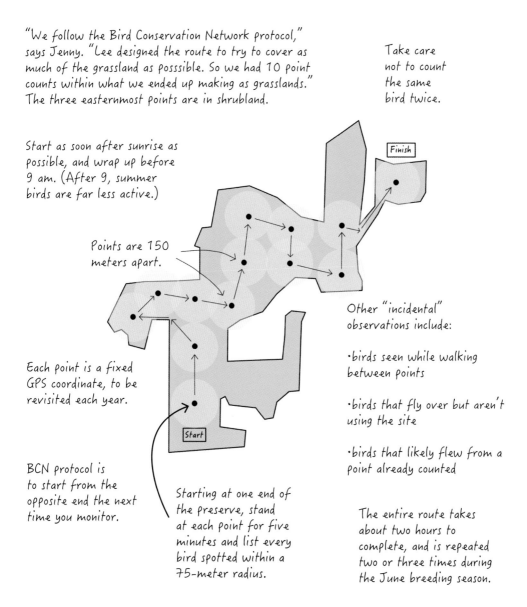

Each point is a fixed GPS coordinate, to be revisited each year.

BCN protocol is to start from the opposite end the next time you monitor.

Starting at one end of the preserve, stand at each point for five minutes and list every bird spotted within a 75-meter radius.

Other "incidental" observations include:

•birds seen while walking between points

•birds that fly over but aren't using the site

•birds that likely flew from a point already counted

The entire route takes about two hours to complete, and is repeated two or three times during the June breeding season.

For more on monitoring, and to learn how to become a bird monitor, visit bcnbirds.org.

Approaching Schaumburg Road

BY JENNY FLEXMAN

In the early years of restoration at Poplar Creek, where the Poplar Creek Prairie Stewards started in 1989, we had to go offsite a lot to get seeds. One of the places we went was Schaumburg Road Grasslands. There were some remnant species down there, so we picked there for about five years. We even burned a fen once or twice. And then, probably for the next 15 years, we never got down there.

In 2009, not everybody in our group was in favor of starting a new project at Schaumburg Road. We already were working on the 300-plus acres of Poplar Creek Prairie, and that required a lot of resources. But the land at Schaumburg Road was only going to get worse if we did nothing. I thought that after 20 years, our group should be striving to make a bigger impact. And I thought we should be able to expand. We had already seeded everything once. So we had the seed resources to broaden our efforts.

At that point, we didn't have a plan other than what Lee had said to us: "Hey, there are grassland birds down here. They're disappearing because of the growth of the hedgerows and shrubs." So we came up with a plan to do what we had been doing at Poplar Creek Prairie, which was to restore the place botanically – but this time with a priority of helping the bird populations.

You had to have a little vision to understand the potential of the grasslands. Walking through it, there was nothing to get excited about. There were no remnants in the prairie; it was mostly Eurasian meadow. On the edges were a couple of little wetland remnants, some remnant fens down in the floodplain, and little pockets in the woods.

We put a lot of thought into seeds. The prevailing theory when we started at Poplar Creek was that you've got to get the aggressive tallgrasses in there first – particularly big bluestem and Indian grass – and they will change the habitat so other species can come in. Since then, people have found that it can take 20 to 40 years or more to get succession from tallgrasses to shorter-statured plants. In the meantime, rank tallgrasses are not conducive to grassland bird populations. So avoiding that problem was in the forefront of our minds. By 2009, other places were having success seeding with a lot less tallgrasses. We ended up taking them out of our mixes completely.

Hedgerows to Henslow's

Over ten years, the Prairie Stewards have reversed the course of shrinking open space at Schaumburg Road Grasslands, and birds have responded.

❶ Hedgerow City

In 1998, Schaumburg Road Grasslands (SRG) was former agricultural land crisscrossed with hedgerows. "It was old fields growing up with lots of shrubs," says Jenny. "There were some natives here and there, but it was mostly Eurasian grasses, autumn olive, and buckthorn." Grassland birds were in decline.

❷ Monitor Birds

Get a pre-restoration baseline, if you can. At SRG, monitors recorded birds from 1998 through 2002. Monitoring resumed in 2009, when restoration began. Each year since, Jenny has monitored two or three times in June. She spends about six hours observing, then "lots of time contemplating what it all means."

❸ Remove Hedgerows

"We focused right away on clearing out shrubs and hedgerows," says Jenny. "That was a fairly lengthy process, four to five years." Eliminate brush strategically: "We removed hedgerows wherever we could expand a field's width enough to matter for the birds," she says (see p. 102).

❹ Burn...

Replace Eurasian old field with native prairie species by burning and seeding. With Forest Preserve crews, Jenny burns only about a third of the prairie annually, since Henslow's sparrows need thatch for nesting. The "extremely complex decision" of how much and where to burn depends on many factors.

❺ ...And Seed

After burning, seed with diverse natives – heavy on the little bluestem and prairie dropseed. The Prairie Stewards' mix excludes big bluestem and Indian grass, which often take over. Burning will weaken turf and make way for new plants, so it's critical to have seed before starting a burn program.

❻ Keep It Open

Follow up regularly for woody resprouts, especially hedgerows, so they don't split up habitat again. Rigorously control invasives such as autumn olive, teasel, reed canary grass, and bird's foot trefoil. Watch for new invaders, too. Mow to control tall goldenrod, but not June 1 through August 15, to avoid disrupting nests. (In general, minimize activity in nest areas during breeding season.)

❼ Overseed

Continue adding seed and plugs to increase native diversity. (Jenny overseeds after burns.) Propagate rarer species. Where big bluestem and Indian grass monocultures were a problem, the Prairie Stewards have knocked them back with prairie dropseed plugs and heavily seeding hemi-parasitic wood betony.

❽ Keep Watching

The longer you monitor, the more trends emerge, and the easier it gets to correlate them with management decisions. After 11 years, grassland bird populations are up, and some species are ongoing indicators of habitat quality.

Birds on the Rise

Years of breeding grassland bird data show promising increases with restoration, but Jenny continues to piece together the complex puzzle of how birds use the landscape.

Peaks and Valleys, but Overall Improvement

Thanks to a cumulative fourteen years of June breeding bird monitoring at Schaumburg Road Grasslands by herself and others, Jenny has a powerful management tool at her disposal: data. One overall trend, at the community level, is already clear: comparing the mean annual aggregate counts of seven obligate grassland bird species before and after restoration began, Jenny's data show a pronounced 263% population increase. (See bar graph, top right.)

The full picture is a complex one Jenny is still working to understand. As the restoration has matured, and more old fields are replaced by prairie, each species has responded differently. Jenny hasn't done a comprehensive analysis yet but has many working theories. "In general," she says, "it seems that it takes a couple of years for birds to find habitat that you make for them."

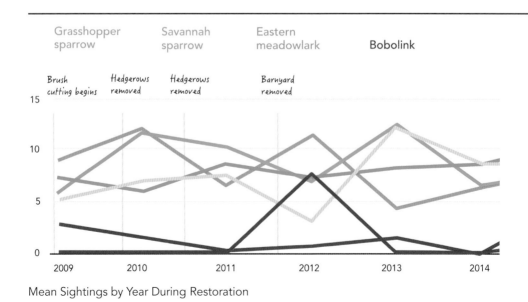

Mean Sightings by Year During Restoration

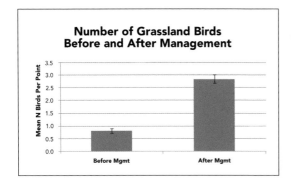

Number of Grassland Birds Before and After Management

Mean aggregate counts of seven grassland species before restoration (1999–2002) and since work began (2009–2019).

The data confirm that the work of the Prairie Stewards and Forest Preserves is headed in the right direction. It has also informed the group's approach to restoring new fields and added context to each new bird sighting.

Among other things, Jenny hopes to separate site trends from regional ones and quantify species-by-species responses to management in specific areas of the site. She's considering factors such as species behavior (for instance, sedge wrens don't nest at SRG until later in the summer, so aren't often captured in June counts) and verifying actual breeding success versus unsuccessful nest attempts. For Jenny, crunching the data is exciting, but it really comes down to what's happening in the field. "It's the excitement of seeing the birds out there," she says. "And then telling people about it, and bringing birders out to see what we've accomplished."

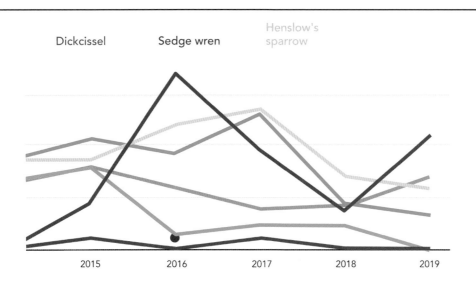

How Birds Are Using the Grasslands

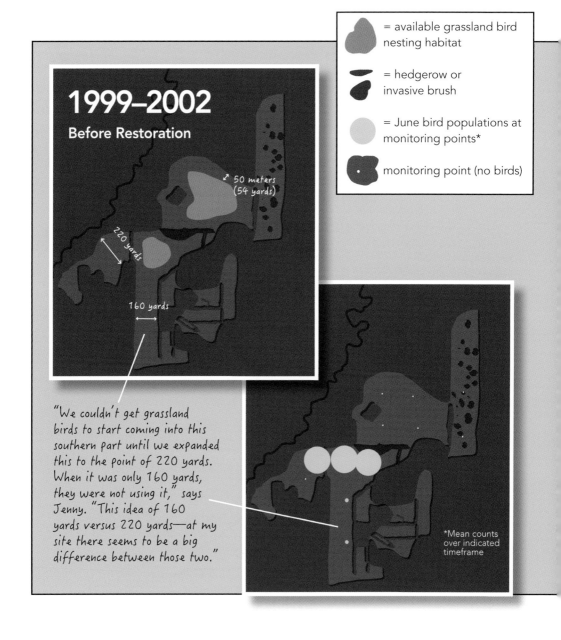

= available grassland bird nesting habitat

= hedgerow or invasive brush

= June bird populations at monitoring points*

monitoring point (no birds)

1999–2002

Before Restoration

↗ 50 meters (54 yards)

220 yards

160 yards

"We couldn't get grassland birds to start coming into this southern part until we expanded this to the point of 220 yards. When it was only 160 yards, they were not using it," says Jenny. "This idea of 160 yards versus 220 yards—at my site there seems to be a big difference between those two."

*Mean counts over indicated timeframe

"The removal of the hedgerows has done wonderful things for the birds out there. It's given me more insights into what their requirements are. **There's more going on than just size or being a certain distance from the woods.**"

— Jenny Flexman

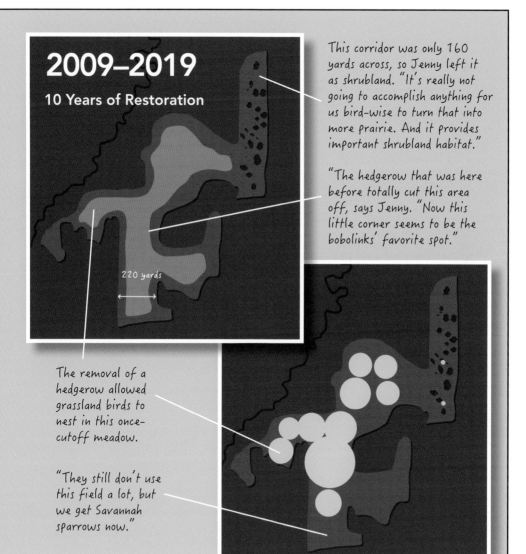

2009–2019

10 Years of Restoration

220 yards

This corridor was only 160 yards across, so Jenny left it as shrubland. "It's really not going to accomplish anything for us bird-wise to turn that into more prairie. And it provides important shrubland habitat."

"The hedgerow that was here before totally cut this area off, says Jenny. "Now this little corner seems to be the bobolinks' favorite spot."

The removal of a hedgerow allowed grassland birds to nest in this once-cutoff meadow.

"They still don't use this field a lot, but we get Savannah sparrows now."

Restoration Takeaways (and Continuing Puzzles)

Jenny and the Prairie Stewards are learning as they go, using emerging science and their own data.

Got Data? You're Way Ahead of the Game

True to her background as an attorney, Jenny has kept detailed records, not just the 10 years of breeding bird surveys (and four before restoration), but also notes of where and when hedgerows and brush were removed, as well as areas burned, seeded, and weeded. Every year, she compiles an annual report. That's a rare thing, and important. It's impossible to do adaptive management without a clear record of what you've done.

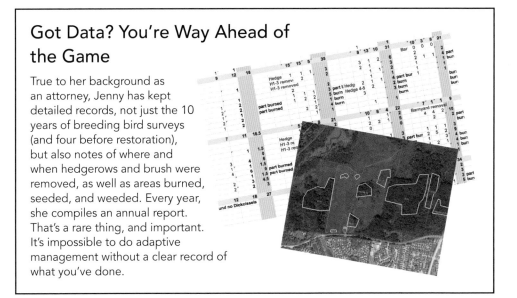

Suite Home Chicago: Taking the Long View on Bird Response

Due to birds' mobility and factors such as conditions on wintering grounds and the rigors of migration, there's a lot of noise in bird data year to year. It can be hard to know what to respond to and where to be patient. Grassland bird populations in restorations frequently show species shifts as a restoration ages, not all pointed upward.

Jenny takes the long view. "Eventually, you're gonna have a very diverse prairie, with lots of plants, short and tall, early blooming, late blooming, grasses, nongrasses, and some of these grassland birds that don't like early restorational fields may end up liking what we do in the long run. So I'm hopeful there."

It may, however, point to opportunities for management innovation. McHenry County Conservation District has shown the highest densities of grasshopper sparrows within their conservation grazing units. This isn't just a question of managing for a single species. The sparrows' absence suggests the disappearance of a historic niche from the landscape. Improving habitat for sparrows could improve habitat for a whole suite of species.

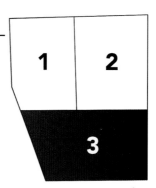

A Formula for Fire?

Jenny and the FPCC try to burn about a third of the prairie with a hot fire each year. But perfecting the burn rotation has been a challenge, in part because a hot burn isn't always possible. If a unit gets a poor burn one year, it may go six years without a good burn, allowing shrubs to grow and shade out the fuel matrix. Jenny started recording not only the quantity but also the quality of burns about six years ago. "I certainly don't have enough data to come to conclusions," she says. She's also exploring the role of more frequent, marginal, patchy, and variable burns.

Seed More Ground Faster

Seed is Jenny's main limiting factor, as it is for many large restorations. Practitioners face a choice: do I seed more acres lightly or fewer acres at a heavier rate? Jenny has kept a seeding rate of about 20 lbs/acre (cleaned seed with rice hulls), but that limits the area she can cover. "Seeding it piece by piece, there's a lot of areas that don't get seeded for a long time, which in one sense is good because it gives you a chance to control thistles and teasel and birdsfoot trefoil, but on the other hand it gives the tall goldenrod a chance to form monocultures. We probably seed 20 acres a year, but ideally, I'd want to do more." What would this take? More hand-collecting? Mechanical harvesting? Purchasing seed?

Tailor Your Seedings

The Prairie Stewards have had success with specialized overseeding, particularly wood betony, which is parasitic on tall grasses. "We've been trying to get wood betony established earlier so it will be there before the tall grasses move in," says Jenny. "You really notice the stature of the plants around it, how short the grasses are there compared to ten feet away." And although Jenny has all but eliminated the use of tall grass seed, around the field edges where birds won't nest and fire won't carry, she's seeded tall grasses to add fuel. In addition, Audubon is planning experiments with new bird-friendly custom seed mixes comprised of short, thin-stemmed natives.

Where Grassland Birds Choose to Nest

As a general rule, grassland birds prefer to nest in open areas of at least 100 acres, and at least 50 meters away from trees. But within that, there's wide variation in moisture, topography, and plant composition that influences the preferences of each species. Over time, Jenny has developed a sense of where to expect grassland nesting birds at Schaumburg Road. Researchers have added to that understanding.

Eastern Meadowlark

Savannah Sparrow

Grasshopper Sparrow

Grasshopper sparrows prefer drier, short, cool-season grasslands with clumps of vegetation. Look for them in recently burned areas and very new restorations. They often drop out within 10 years of restoration.

The least area-dependent of the grassland-obligate species, Savannah sparrows will nest near brush. They prefer shorter grass. Less secretive than other grassland sparrows.

Grassland generalists, eastern meadowlarks will nest in a variety of vegetation heights.

Bobolinks are flexible, with an affinity for mesic, medium-height, medium-density Eurasian cool-season meadows. Managers are now trying to find mixes of native species that will support high levels of bobolinks.

(Birds enlarged to show detail.)

Bobolink

Dickcissel

Sedge Wren

Henslow's Sparrow

One of the least reliable indicators of local habitat quality, dickcissels may show up intermittently in grasslands, particularly mid-height mesic restorations.

Sedge wrens can often be found in wetter areas with denser vegetation, so listen for their staccato song near wetlands.

Happy to breed in both cool-season and warm-season grasslands, the Henslow's sparrow prefers tall grass and needs thick, unburned thatch from previous years' growth. When planning prescribed fire, leave some areas unburned for Henslow's.

Sources: State of the Grasslands: Chicago Wilderness – 2018, National Audubon Society and Illinois Audubon Society. Cindy Jablonski, McHenry County Conservation District.

A Legacy of Listening

Many birders find the prospect of birding by ear daunting, but Jenny sees it as a way in. "You hear a blue jay or a crow and you know what it is, okay?" she says. "It's fairly distinctive and you've never really put any thought into it. Our bodies are wired to learn things by sound."

Acoustic ecologist Gordon Hempton agrees. As he recounted to *On Being* in 2012, birds have been sharing ecological information with us for thousands of generations.

Several years ago, Hempton was trying to solve a puzzle. His linguist colleagues believed that human hearing evolved to enable storytelling and coordinated, person-to-person work. Yet if that's true, he wondered, why is it that humans have super-hearing at a range well above what the human voice can produce?

Hempton started investigating what in the ancestral environment correlated with that range – between 2.5 and 5 kilohertz – where our super-hearing lives. He found a perfect fit in birdsong. But why?

Though we are visual creatures, sight has its limitations. Sure, on a clear day with long sight lines, a person can see for miles, but what about on a foggy morning in a shrubland? And in how many directions can you see at one time? At what range can you glean detailed information about what is around you? Now, almost regardless of the weather, how far can you hear? And in how many directions simultaneously? Hempton says he's been able to hear sounds as far as 20 miles away. Applying that in every direction, our ears theoretically have the ability to survey an area of 1,276 square miles in an instant.

Hempton concluded that birds exponentially increased the area early humans were able to monitor and understand. The distant Louisiana waterthrush told us a stream was nearby. The scold of a blue jay betrayed some big animal on the move. The metallic belch of the brown-headed cowbird signaled bison beyond the next rise. For hundreds of thousands of years, birds likely helped humans navigate a landscape we couldn't fully see our way through.

That ability hasn't disappeared. We are far better with our ears than we think. And with a bit of practice, stewards can leverage this evolutionary heritage and let sound-producing wildlife – not just birds, but frogs, singing insects, and more – tell us more about what in our restorations is working and what's not.

Getting More Eyes on What Flies

Jenny on how — and why — to fledge more steward-monitors.

As we work to increase bird populations, how do we increase the population of bird *people*?

"I know BCN works really hard at getting monitors," says Jenny, "but it can be a challenge. Maybe we need to look in some new places."

"I've always assumed that bird monitors come from birders," says Jenny. "But if this is a simple, learnable process, maybe we should be trying to train people who are already volunteering at these sites. Maybe we're ignoring a whole population of people who would be interested in monitoring. It'd be a lot easier for somebody to learn how to monitor birds than it would be for them to learn how to monitor plants."

"The stewards and volunteers are going to have that initial tie to the site," she says, "and better understand why certain management actions are being taken, or why one bird population may decline in favor of another." On the other hand, the right birder may develop a genuine, nuanced attachment to the site, too.

"If you can get a steward to start monitoring, I don't know how they would not get more interested in the birds," says Jenny. "They're gonna want to understand *why is this bird doing this? Why didn't we see this bird this year?* And they'll incorporate it into their thinking and their management. That's kind of what happened with me. I don't think I would've become a monitor if I hadn't started the restoration project. Once I started doing it, my interest in birds snowballed."

Tips for Making Fledgling Monitors

Get a Mentor (Or Be One)

For Jenny, the one-on-one experience of a close mentorship was the key to transformation. "Lee Ramsey was my mentor. I hadn't been a monitor before. I wasn't, by any means, an expert on identification of grassland birds at the time," she says. "Lee would go out in the field with me. He was one of the co-leaders of the BCN at the time, so he was spending a lot of time mentoring people – I wasn't the only person. He was spending a lot of time in the field already. So he was trying to pass it on to me."

Connect to Resources

There is a wealth of digital resources available to aspiring bird monitors. The Cornell Lab of Ornithology (CLO) has several useful free apps. Their eBird app allows for streamlined data collection in the field. The largest, most successful citizen-science effort on the planet, eBird (ebird.org) is a powerful tool to track species trends based on more than 100 million sightings submitted each year by eBird's hundreds of thousands of users. From the website, birders can explore data, including from areas they plan to visit, and see which species have been reported. Merlin, CLO's bird ID app, is based on eBird data and even includes ID-from-photo capabilities. Numerous excellent digital field guides are also available. Sibley Birds, for example, is easy to use and includes species descriptions, range maps, songs and calls, as well as David Sibley's original art.

Get in the Field

"I'm realizing that seeing is believing for stewards and volunteers," says Jenny, "not just hearing from me, not just seeing data, and not just knowing that the birds are important. We did a site walk this year for the volunteer leaders. Luckily we had a big turnout, and we had two pileated woodpeckers show up. It was the best way to sell people on protecting dead trees! We need to do more than an occasional woodcock or owl walk if we want volunteers to get interested in birds."

Start Easy

"The other thing to get folks to start monitoring grassland birds is convincing them there's not that many birds to learn. You know, there's all kinds of stuff that can be in the woods! But in grasslands, you only have to learn six or seven birds. And so you have to convince them that this isn't going to be that hard to pick up on."

Beyond Birds

Can I monitor more taxa?

To really understand a site, you'd need to monitor every living creature that walks, crawls, slithers, or flies. But for those muttering to themselves that there would need to be twenty of me to do all of that, here are a few ideas.

Just add one new group

What do you most want to know about? What's most likely to inform what you do on the land? Where does your curiosity lead? Make it a "stretch goal" to monitor just one new taxon. "Wherever you're at now, do a little bit more, and you'll be doing more," says steward and monitoring mentor Karen Glennemeier. "And then come back again in a couple years and maybe you can do a little more." In addition to birds, Schaumburg Road volunteers now keep tabs on butterflies, bees, dragonflies, and damselflies.

Call on community

At its best, natural areas stewardship isn't a solo endeavor. Our networks of agency staff and volunteers can back one another up and contribute skills and knowledge. Find out whether there are already monitors surveying your site that may be a ready source of data -- ask your landholder's regional ecologist or the groups on the facing page. If there aren't already monitors at your site, inquire about having someone adopt your site. Then establish a working relationship with regular check-ins to get the most from what they're learning. The more taxa you add, the better. Imagine walking laps of your preserve with a different expert each time!

Stack your taxa

Running what might be the Cadillac of wildlife monitoring programs, Lake County Forest Preserves biologists sample multiple taxa at each of 235 monitoring points throughout the county. On land, they record mammals, birds, and herps at each point against a backdrop of natural communities. More detailed plant monitoring is now being discussed. Aquatic points document fish, herps, and crayfish and will soon also include mussels and other aquatic invertebrates. "The goal is to properly categorize each area to better understand how the community changes over time, including how they are affected by our management," says wildlife ecologist Gary Glowacki. "By including multiple taxa, we have a better view into the complex ecosystems we are working to conserve."

Wildlife Monitoring Resources

Bird Conservation Network

This all-volunteer coalition has long been the leader for coordinated bird monitoring and analysis in the Chicago region. Its cohort of monitors collects and reports on data across hundreds of sites – and they're always looking for more. bcnbirds.org

Illinois Butterfly Monitoring Network

Since 1987, this citizen-science program has grown from seven to more than 100 routes, tallying butterflies to understand longterm trends on public natural lands, particularly in response to management. Based at the Chicago Academy of Science's Peggy Notebaert Nature Museum, and more recently joined by the Calling Frog Survey and Illinois Odonate Survey. bfly.org

Calling Frog Survey

Since 2000, the Calling Frog Survey has trained regular citizens in the Chicago region to venture out to wetlands and count frogs and toads calling for mates. frogsurvey.org

Illinois Odonate Survey

Originally added to the Chicago-region monitoring universe as the Dragonfly Monitoring Network, the Illinois Odonate Survey (IOS) specializes in dragonflies and damselflies. illlinoisodes.org

Illinois RiverWatch

With a decidedly terrestrial focus, many restorations overlook aquatic environments. If your site has a wadeable stream, it may be a candidate for monitoring (or already be adopted) through RiverWatch, a program designed to track the quality of Illinois waterways. The monitoring protocol includes macroinvertebrate and habitat surveys. ngrrec.org/riverwatch

The Future

Toward a Larger Vision

Driving most of the stewardship decisions Jenny and the Poplar Creek Prairie Stewards make is a much larger vision. "The District bought the 4,200 acres now called Arthur Janura Forest Preserve in the late '60s, early '70s," says Jenny. From 1989 to 2009, Forest Preserves of Cook County volunteers, with staff support, transformed the northwest corner. "What we had accomplished in 20 years was amazing," says Jenny. "For volunteers to take five acres

and turn it into a 250-acre prairie, with the diversity that we had in there, I think was phenomenal. But we'd only done 250 acres." So they expanded to Schaumburg Road, adding about 200 acres of prairie, as well as more than 200 acres of woods and wetlands.

But Schaumburg Road was just the next step. "If you go eastward, there are at least 3,000 more acres of what should be prairie," she says. "We can't let this sit there forever... So that's why I felt it was time to expand and think long-term. And the big, long-term vision is a massive prairie, bigger than Orland Grasslands, that would hold untold numbers of grassland birds, including being sufficiently large to have northern harriers and short-eared owls." Making that vision a reality will be a long road of conversations, planning, constituency building, and continued restoration. The Prairie Stewards welcome the challenge – with the birds guiding the way.

Satellite image: Google, Landsat / Copernicus

Notes

About Jenny Flexman

Jenny Flexman is volunteer site steward of Schaumburg Road Grasslands and the leader of the Poplar Creek Prairie Stewards. Over her 31 years in habitat restoration, she has served on multiple county-wide stewardship committees.

"I grew up with a father who took us camping five weeks a year," says Jenny. In 1989, she discovered habitat restoration. "I was kind of at a point where I was taking charge of my life. I quit my job and started my own law practice. But I also wanted to give back to the world environmentally. I had very few clients at the time, so I called up The Nature Conservancy and I asked them if they needed any free legal services." They didn't, but they pointed Jenny to a volunteer fair on a beautiful fall day at Crabtree Nature Center. "I found that really kind of idyllic," she says. There she learned about the Poplar Creek Prairie Stewards group, then just two months old.

Jenny volunteered for decades, helping to restore the grassland at Poplar Creek (aka Carl Hansen Forest Preserve). Early on, steward Rick McAndless asked her to lead seed collection at the site's high-quality hill prairie. "I said yes, as I tend to do," she says. "But I just wasn't one to sit out with a book and key things out a lot. Taking on that job forced me to do it. And so for a year, I was probably out at Shoe Factory Road Nature Preserve at least once a week for a few hours, book in hand, watching the plants as they progressed from flowering to seed, and identifying things. That was what really gave me the knowledge to go down the path of being a leader."

Quercus macrocarpa 14/85 2015   C. Carlson

"I was so thankful that not only did The Nature Conservancy hook me up with Poplar Creek, but also that they didn't take me up on my offer to do legal services," says Jenny. "Because ultimately, in my life, I did not need more reasons to be indoors. I needed reasons to be outdoors."

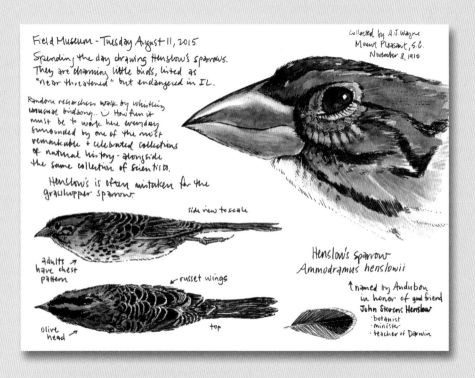

Field Museum - Tuesday August 11, 2015

Spending the day drawing Henslow's sparrows. They are charming little birds, listed as "near threatened" but endangered in IL.

Random researchers walk by whistling unusual birdsong... ♡ How fun it must be to work here everyday surrounded by one of the most remarkable + celebrated collections of natural history - alongside the same collection of scientists.

Henslow's is often mistaken for the grasshopper sparrow.

Collected by A.J. Wayne
Mount Pleasant, S.C.
November 8, 1910

side view to scale

adults ↗ have chest pattern

← russet wings

olive head ↗

top

Henslow's sparrow
Ammodramus henslowii

↑ named by Audubon
in honor of good friend
John Stevens Henslow
· botanist
· minister
· teacher of Darwin

The Society of Stewardship

with Stephen Packard, Linda Masters, and Eriko Kojima

Habitat restoration hinges on successful human communities. While it's not always easy, we're never alone.

When steward Stephen Packard crosses the street into Somme Prairie Grove, everything shifts. "I often hum this little song that starts, *Heaven, I'm in heaven...*," he sings. "And sometimes I say, 'Oh, I'm too busy' or 'I wonder if I should go somewhere else.' And whenever I'm there, I just say, 'Ohhhhhh. It's so wonderful.' I love going over and discovering new things that have transpired. More and more rare plants and animals are there all the time. I go and monitor, I go count all the savanna blazing stars.... 'Oh wow, look at that one! Oh, they've never been here before!' And it's this wonderful discovery – nature is doing this, and we're facilitating, and it's happening."

When we hear the word "steward," it's this sort of joyful and intensely personal experience that most of us probably think of. In the context of Chicago-region habitat restoration, "steward" evokes an unusually dedicated person who spends decades on a site, learning the plants and studying the landscape.

But as the volunteer site steward of Somme Prairie Grove, a leader for more than 43 years of the North Branch Restoration Project, and catalyst for scores of other groups, Stephen has learned that successful restoration – on the scale it is really needed – is a highly social, collaborative activity. Like it or not, stewards usually find themselves at the heart of a group's culture, leading workdays, wrangling committees, organizing social events. And, it turns out, many stewards come to find the social aspects as rewarding as (and completely intertwined with) the ecological ones. Stephen now considers his restoration colleagues family.

Stewardship is complicated. There's a lot to know. It requires diverse skills, from the botanical to the logistical to the interpersonal. A steward has to be both ecological and social manager, able to develop his or her understanding of the land while empowering a group and building its culture. There are rarely one-size-fits-all answers, but in this chapter,

A happy winter workday on the North Branch.

Stephen, along with Somme Woods site steward Linda Masters and Somme steward Eriko Kojima, share their own experiences.

New generations of leaders are critical to sustaining communities that care for our natural places over the long term. There's a growing need for new stewards. Young volunteers participate regularly, yet many groups still look to leaders who began this work almost a half century ago. Ideally, we will preserve essential traditions while sparking new initiatives, start groups where needed, and continually reinvent the way we work and whom we include.

While Stephen, Linda, and Eriko share things that have worked, the point is not to lead exactly like them. It's to find your place in this multifaceted community and lead in a way that's genuine for you.

We are not alone in this work. The society of stewardship extends far beyond our present community of caretakers, professional and volunteer. Knowledge of how and why to preserve the land has been passed down from many who came before – the Committee on the Universe, Friends of Our Native Landscape, the Prairie Club, Leopold, Watts, Turner, Swink, Schulenberg, Betz, and the Wades, to name just a few (and to say too little of the American Indian cultures who built their knowledge over millennia). We risk losing our accumulated wisdom, to say nothing of our native ecosystems, if we lose the longer, wider view.

"It's in the culture that we should take care of the planet," says Stephen. People are constantly stepping up to help grow that culture. With any luck, it will play a role in restoring humanity's relationship with nature long after we're gone.

Catalyzing Conservation Culture

A network of restoration groups, each different from the other, thrives across Chicago Wilderness. But they didn't happen by accident.

Influenced by conservaton pioneers from Aldo Leopold, May Theilgaard Watts, and George Fell to Robert Betz and Ray Schulenberg, Stephen Packard has spent half his life identifying would-be volunteer leaders and connecting them with needy tracts in Cook County forest preserves and beyond. Since the mid-1970s, he has recruited thousands of volunteers, empowered new stewards, and helped establish human communities restoring the land's biodiversity. It's one of the things he works harder on than almost anyone else.

Stephen will insist that these groups built themselves – and he's not wrong. Yet he was a catalyst common to so many of them. Both professionally and as a volunteer, he worked with dozens of groups restoring more than 100 sites – a considerable percentage of those still active today. Rather than directing or controlling, he set off chain reactions.

The number of volunteer hours dedicated to natural areas by these groups is staggering – hundreds of thousands of hours through the decades. But just as impressive are the lives touched, expertise developed, and connections made to the land. Each of these groups is a universe in itself, with its own practices and traditions. Drop in on any two to see how they work, and you'll find they have very distinct personalities. Yet they share a common culture too, often comparing notes and gathering for inspiration.

Some groups, not on this list, died out after a year or two. (Tip: When lighting a brushpile, touch your match in several places – some catch, some fizzle out.) Groups do start spontaneously, but many are the result of intention and deliberate organizing. To sustain citizen-fueled restoration, others may have to pick up the torch and light new fires.

❶ North Branch Restoration Project
Est. 1977
Originally the North Branch Prairie Project, this group has become a model for volunteer-based restoration in the Chicago region and beyond. The group manages 22 sites along the North Branch of the Chicago River, from Northbrook south to the Northwest Side of Chicago.

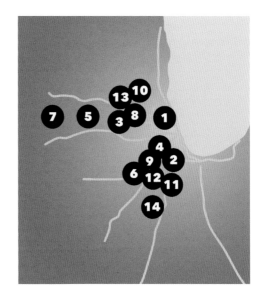

❷ South Suburban Prairie Project
Est. 1980
Thrived for decades, but crashed during the mid-1990s restoration moratorium.

❸ Friends of Bluff Spring Fen
Est. 1980
Longtime stewards manage this rare but once-abused Illinois Nature Preserve.

❹ Des Plaines River Valley Restoration Project
Est. 1983
Founding leaders restored rare dolomite prairie at Ted Stone Preserve and other sites.

❺ Kane County Natural Areas Volunteers
Est. 1983
Steward June Keibler helped launch several groups across Kane County.

❻ Old Plank Road Prairie Stewards
Est. 1984
Cared for 21-mile prairie along former railroad in south suburbs. Group faded, but site now adopted by Orland Volunteers.

❼ Nachusa Grasslands Volunteers
Est. 1986
Unique symbiosis between TNC staff and volunteers restoring 4,000+ acres.

❽ Poplar Creek Prairie Stewards
Est. 1989
Classic kick-off spawned thriving group.

❾ Palos Restoration Project
Est. 1990
Loose affiliation of stewards focus on priority sites in 15,000-acre complex.

❿ Deer Grove Natural Areas Volunteers
Est. 1995
Restoring the core plant communities in Cook County's first preserve.

⓫ Bartel Grassland Volunteers
Est. 2000
Large-scale, volunteer-fueled restoration of 585-acre grassland.

⓬ Orland Grassland Volunteers
Est. 2002
PR-oriented steward Pat Hayes keeps work in the public eye at 960-acre site.

⓭ Spring Creek Stewards
Est. 2003
Tackling a 4,000-acre site by dividing stewardship into several smaller areas.

⓮ Friends of Langham Island
Est. 2014
Launched to save the exceedingly rare Kankakee mallow and its river sanctuary.

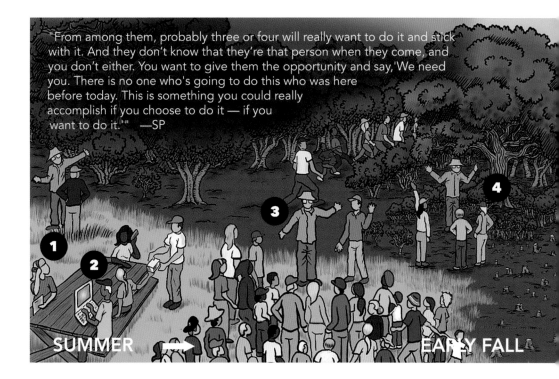

"From among them, probably three or four will really want to do it and stick with it. And they don't know that they're that person when they come, and you don't either. You want to give them the opportunity and say, 'We need you. There is no one who's going to do this who was here before today. This is something you could really accomplish if you choose to do it — if you want to do it.'" —SP

SUMMER ➡ EARLY FALL

Launching a New Group

Stephen Packard's proven method relies on starting with a big bang and never losing momentum. It also works for relaunches.

❶ Get the Landowner On Board
"The first thing you need is a landowner who wants to empower people," says Stephen, who has helped kickstart many groups over decades, including the auspicious launch of the Poplar Creek Prairie Stewards.

❷ Invite the World
"Every time I've started one of these groups," he says, "we've started with a bang, a big event. Invite the world. Put out as much PR as you can. Sometimes everyone comes from an article. Sometimes everyone comes from Sierra Club or The Nature Conservancy. Sometimes it's the network of people who talk to people who talk to people." Reach out personally, and use the planning process to get a smart, committed group of co-conspirators on board early.

❸ Kickoff Event
With luck, you'll get 25 to 100 people. Speeches and displays should leave people wanting more. "It has been great when we have an important person there representing some major institution who says, 'This is important.'" Professor Robert Betz was one such person, inspiring groups with a vision of prairies growing "ever richer, more beautiful, more important, more worthy of your pride."

❹ Ask For Leaders

"Since you can't have a discussion with 80 people at once, at Poplar Creek I asked, 'Who'd be interested in helping learn to lead?' A dozen people raised hands. I said, 'Okay great. Meet me over by that tree.' We stood there for a half hour talking, and then someone said, 'I'll edit the newsletter.' 'I've done brush cutting.' 'I'll do seeds.'" Co-leaders can lead the other attendees on site tours.

❺ Begin Work ASAP

Start workdays within a week or two. Holding the kickoff in early fall or spring leaves a window of fair weather for new volunteers to gain their footing. Keep up the frequency — weekly or biweekly events keep up group interest.

❻ Training Wheels

An experienced steward-organizer is essential early on. He or she can offer ecology advice, talk to the landowner, and help volunteers learn to take charge. While a big job at first (every weekend for months), this organizing becomes less and less necessary. "The group has to set its sights much higher than what one person can do," says Stephen, "so real leadership is needed from new leaders."

❼ Keep On Going

A well-established project will see fluctuations over the years, but "not in the commitment and confidence of the volunteer congregation," says Stephen. "Leaders will evolve and change. New people will join, and the consistent motivator and reward is the ecosystem. With dedication, natural communities get richer and healthier year after year."

A Living Congregation

Build your volunteer group for the long haul.

The Land Needs a Lasting Congregation

To anyone who has followed politics, looked at marriage statistics, or tried to start a band, the prospect of creating lasting human communities with a sustained focus may sound daunting. Yet to achieve meaningful and lasting ecosystem restoration, the human community that cares for a bit of land must last decades, even centuries. "Just like a church has a congregation and they support it over the years, these places need to have congregations," says Stephen. He has likened restoration to building a cathedral over generations, where those who start the work know they won't get to see it finished, but do it anyway. "I had the sense that this is sort of an organism, you just have to kind of keep it going, and people will end up joining in and moving it forward."

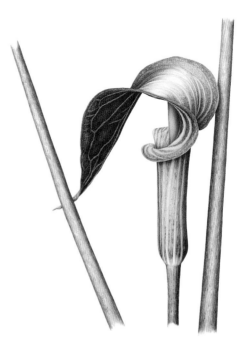

"There's no point in doing this for five years or ten years and stopping," he says. "Then you might as well not have done it."

A Successful Group Is a Highly Social Organism

To inaccurately paraphrase Charlton Heston circa 1973, "Restoration is people! It's made out of people!!!" A visiting colleague of Stephen's reported that he assumed volunteer habitat restoration was going to be 90 percent about the ecosystem and 10 percent about the people. After touring sites with Stephen, he realized he'd gotten that backwards. Restoration requires an army of hands to cut, pull, pick, and sow, of course, but it goes much deeper than that. Stephen points to environmental philosopher Bill Jordan, who writes, "Human beings are social species. For such a species, relationship with nature is not a personal matter, but is necessarily mediated by the community."

We primates need each other. We need each other's brawn, but also shared knowledge and wisdom, techniques for survival and success, emotional and spiritual support. That's all in play within a volunteer group. "It's so hard for me to tease apart the human factors from the skills and the functional stuff," says Eriko.

**"There's no point in doing this for
five years or ten years and stopping.
Then you might as well not have done it."**

The North Branch Restoration Project
has been intentionally social since the
beginning, with lunches together in the field
and workdays ending with pie and coffee
at Poppin' Fresh Pies. Even activities that
have nothing to do with restoration can
benefit the work. "Chris Hodak did this
very important thing," says Stephen. "She
organized the International Supper Club –
three couples from the North Branch who
went out to ethnic restaurants one night a
week. And they developed a coherence... I
mean, they became an important leadership
part of this."

For Resilience, Build in Diversity and Redundancy

"We want diversity of people, not only the
biodiversity in the ecosystem," says Eriko.
"Ethnic or racial, religious diversity, but also
diversity of ages, life stages, educational levels,
everything. We don't want to just aim for a
sweet spot of younger people or retired people.
Any organization or organism is more robust
when you've got diversity."

Building a large roster of people in many
different situations – both active volunteers
and those in the "reserves" – has paid off
for the longest-lasting volunteer groups. "I
think that a lot of the younger people who are
not committing yet, maybe in the end when
they're in a more stable time in their life, will be
stewards," says Eriko. "And it might take years.
Just like Rob Sulski, right? Took him 20 years
to start growing plants. So it just incubates in
your heart. You know, you just have this nice
feeling about it and this commitment at the level
that you can at that time."

Assemble a Tribe of Doers

Just like in a hunter-gatherer group, specialization and complementary skills are key to effectiveness — and even survival.

Stephen has spent a long time considering teamwork in restoration. "Think of these groups as hunter-gatherer groups," he says. "We humans, we have very different strengths from person to person. Somebody is good at math; somebody is good at geography – they know how to get from place to place; we have people who are physically good hunters; we have people who nurture stuff, growing little things; we have people who help the group process. And we need them all."

Some skills are indispensable. "Inspiring people to know the plants is just a key thing," says Stephen. "And you don't have to learn everything, but you have to get excited about starting to learn."

Having leaders with basic restoration experience is critical too. Focusing on a specialty may help volunteers develop expertise faster. "If there are three of you," says Stephen, "maybe one person learns the plants, one person learns herbicide and forestry techniques, and the other one learns seeds. In one person, or in a number of people, you need all this stuff."

But having technical or "hard skills" isn't enough. "There are people in all the stewardship groups who are technically good, and that alone doesn't do it," says Stephen. "Now there are also people who are the mom or the dad of the group, and help people get along with each other, and maintain the spirit,

etcetera, which is critical.... A lot of times, there's sort of a social person who ends up being the principal glue for the larger group."

Success hinges in large part around empowering volunteers – supporting them, but mostly getting out of their way. "A lot of this is dependent on independent people who have independent ideas," says Stephen. "Our first person along these lines was Preston Spinx, who decided to grow rows of rare prairie plants between his beans and cabbages in his little garden in his Morton Grove backyard. The Botanic Garden couldn't get hoary puccoon to grow, but he could get it to grow because he just gave it a lot of attention.... And he did that with a bunch of plants."

Another case of specialization in the North Branch was Gail Schmoller. "She was not a workday type – she was much more of a high heels and fancy clothes type. But she had decided that she would like to create a career for herself as a public relations person. And she said, 'I've been reading about you in the paper. Could I publicize you, to gain experience and get contacts and demonstrate that I'm good at it?' So she adopted us.... And a huge portion of our success came from Gail Schmoller getting us into the media all the time."

A diverse group can mean fresh ideas that move a group forward, says Linda. "Somebody will come in and be oblivious to all the politics and say, 'I've

Somme Prairie Grove

Home
Maps
News
Volunteering
- How To Volunteer
- Workday Schedule
- Volunteer Roles
- Habitat Heroes
- Meet the Volunteers
- Photo Stories
  - A Fine Work Party
  - A Good Spring Burn
  - Winter Solstice Celebration
Guides
Ecology
Resources

Find current photos and info tidbits at **Friends of Somme Preserve** in Facebook.

Check out more detailed stories on Somme plants, wildlife, fun, and beauty on the **Vestal Grove Blog**.

More technical Somme stories can be found on the **Strategies for Stewards Blog**.

Habitat Heroes

The list below is very partial. Literally hundreds of people deserve credit. may give you a sense of the scope of the work — and maybe even ideas contributions they might make.

Researchers and Monitors:
Birds: Jerry Sullivan, Ben Risk, Judy Pollock
Butterflies: Jeff Sanders and Joan Palincsar
Endangered plants: Kevin Clay, Andrea Tietmeyer, Joe Walsh
Insect communities: Ron Panzer
Frogs: Karen Glennemeier, Joe Walsh
Mammals: Steve Byers
Plant communities: Marlin Bowles, John and Jane Balaban, Jerry Wilhelm, John Johnson

Seed Gatherers: Joan Meersman, Laurel Ross, Paul Dolinko, Duke Riggen Ross Sweeny, Hollis Baker, Rufino Osorio, Linda Masters, and many, many

Brush Bashers: Michael Heyman, Rhett Donnelley, Joe Walsh, Dennis Debra Shore, Pete Baldo, Ross Sweeny, Eileen Sutter, Marianne Kozlowski

Weed Wallopers: Donna Hriljac, Debra Shore, Kent Fuller, Kevin Clay

Master Gardeners: Preston Spinks, David Sollenburger

Perimeter Defense Watchman and Advocate: Wally Johnson

Trails Blazers and Maintainers: Andy Smith

Artists, Publicists and Writers: Marlene Hill Donnelley, Bobby Sutton, Laurel Ross, Jerry Sullivan, Cynthia Gehrie, Bill Kurtis, William K. Stevens Siewers

Recruiters and Spirit Boosters: Nancy Freehaffer, Karen Holland, Rob Kampwirth, Fr. Jay Risk, Derek Supple, Rebecca Blazer, Joe Walsh, Jerri

Mighty Acorns (youth stewardship) organizers: Julie Sacco, Sue Ke

Chicago Wilderness Rangers organizers: Richard Day, Lauren Willia

Organizers and planners: Stephen Packard, John and Jane Balaban, Beverley Hansen, Linda Masters, Kelly Trease, Steve Thomas, Bill Koenig

Hallowed restoration advisors: Dr. Robert Betz, Ray Schulenburg, Taron, Ken Mierzwa, Judy Pollock

Historic inspirers and guides: Henry Thoreau, Aldo Leopold, Ted Sperry

For years, a page on Stephen's Somme Prairie Grove website credited the contributions of a wide range of people, past and present.

got this great idea, and I'm just gonna do it!' And they'll do it, and the fallout will happen, and it'll be a success." Many worthy projects happen this way, she says. "It really needs that spark-plug person to grab ahold of it."

There's a role for every member to play, says Stephen. "There are people who, for example, have kids or they've gotten older, and they just can't get out of the house as much, but they would love to do something from home."

Sometimes all it takes to fill the holes and round out your group is to make it known there's a need. "One thing we don't do enough is to get that list of who's doing what and what's needed out widely very often," says Stephen, "which would be a good thing for us to do."

The Complete Steward*ship*

Whether in a single steward or spread across a group, there are some key roles that most groups need to fill.

Successful volunteer restorations have many moving parts, some obvious, some behind the scenes. In the early stages of a group, all this work might be done by one person, or a few. As the community develops, more and more people will pitch in (if the "leaders" let them), and growth and specialization follow. Having a ready list of roles may help stewards think about how to actively welcome people's contributions.

Watchman

Eyes on the ground. Always in the field, knows what's going on, identifies emerging issues. Protects against poaching, vandalism, emerging invasives. Helps visitors.

Ecologist

Understands and studies the land, plants, and animals, and what needs to be done to restore it. Makes main ecological decisions, including working with landowner to create a management plan. Constantly scouting. What most people mean when they say "steward."

Technician

Gets the physical restoration work done — sawing, lopping, herbiciding, seed collecting, plug planting, burning. Has their chainsaw certification. Shows by doing, and sets an example of good, hard work.

Mechanic

Maintains a group's tools, keeping the toolshed well organized, saws sharp, herbicide mixed, and everything ready to go at 8:30 on a Saturday morning.

10-IN-1!

Welcomer

Literally welcomes people at workdays, setting a friendly, inclusive tone. Always inviting people to join in, whether at a grocery store or a natural area. Makes sure volunteers are comfortable, answers questions, shares tips, finds out what they're interested in.

Visionary

Takes the long view and keeps an inspiring vision in front of the group, not only for the site but for ecological restoration in the region and beyond.

AUTHENTIC MULTIPURPOSE UTILITY STEWARDSHIP TOOL

Connector

Connects the group to the community. Liaises with landowner staff, and meets with community members. May organize advocacy or activism in response to opportunities and threats. May serve as group figurehead.

Convener

Plans and organizes events, from workdays to social outings. Responsible for the logistical nuts and bolts, including people-wrangling, that make things go smoothly.

Interpreter

Introduces people to the natural world, including teaching plant and wildlife ID. Tells the story of a place and shows volunteers how to read the landscape. May serve as group reference librarian, keeping historical records, giving context for the work.

Communicator

Writes emails, organizes newsletter, active on social media. Shares the story of the volunteers and the work both internally and with a wider audience, including with media. May be a group's tech person or webmaster.

Patterns of Leadership

Restoration needs leaders. But leadership isn't reserved for boss types or plant savants — there are many paradigms, and all kinds can lead.

The Collective Model

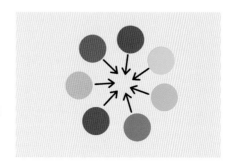

"There are two very different types of groups," says Stephen. "It goes one way or the other way. One way is the charismatic, dominating leader. The other is the group leader. And I always work as hard as I can to encourage potential 'strong leader' folks to accept and encourage collectivity."

The collective, facilitative approach proved a good fit for the North Branch, but it was something Stephen had to learn. "I came from The Movement of the '60s, where there was this vision of participatory democracy and collectivity," he says. "And it was frowned on to have a leader in charge of stuff. And I'd worked in these groups...and I'd seen people who were effective and people who weren't. And I wonder if it came as an advantage to me. I was a deeply unsocial person before I got involved in that stuff. I found it difficult to talk to people. I was much more likely to sit around feeling crabby about everyone else than engage in give-and-take. And I learned sociability in that society."

"In some ways, the key is a leader who's accepting," says Stephen. "The person that is more of a leader than a boss has to appreciate people who have great stuff to offer, and who want to do it their own way, and help them figure out how their own way can work in this context."

The Top-Down Model

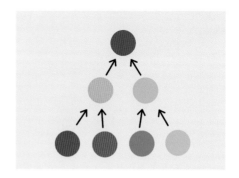

Sometimes groups develop with a single prominent leader who does most key decision making, gives directions, and keeps things moving forward. "People take this very seriously, and they really want to do a good job," says Stephen. "And for many people that means, 'I want to control every bit.' They don't think of themselves as controlling, they just think it has to be done a certain exact way."

There have been successful examples of restoration leaders in this mold, says Stephen, but he doesn't see it as best. "Groups driven too much by a single person sometimes die and end," he says. "I've seen that happen. Whereas if it's more of a community, then it keeps going."

"Leaders will come and go," says Linda. "Pastors and priests will come and go. But if you have a congregation..."

Steward Teams

Some groups have multiple heads — a duo or perhaps a close-knit team who make key decisions together. "I remember one wonderful group that started with two clear leaders," says Stephen. "I mean, there were many leaders of many different parts of it, but two people were sort of the central leaders. And one of them was the technique, science, workday leader. And the other was the human potential leader — the newsletter, parties,

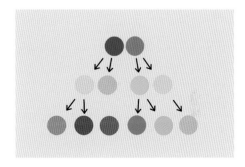

recruiting, welcoming new people, etc. And they got along very well, and they worked very well together, until some people started Chairman Mao-ifying one of the leaders. And all of a sudden the publication started to be full of 'Oh, this person is so wonderful, we would be nowhere without this person,' and so I thought that hurt. And the other person dropped out."

Stephen recounts another leader pair. "Organizing the biggest, best early prairie conference, there were these two women who were the leaders of it. And the first person, who was really smart, creative, talented, and not a boss kind of person, said, 'Organizations do well if they're led by two people, one of whom is the searching, creative, looking-every-direction, finding-new-stuff kind of person, and the other person is the control person.' The other person says, 'Everything has to be in control, and I have to make sure....' And the first person says, 'Yeah, great! That's not me!' But if they really like and get along with each other, then you have a great company or a great organization."

Leading from the Ranks

Leadership can be found in many other places besides the top of the org chart. People lead from within organizations all the time, whether directing their own project or sparking great ideas. Others lead simply by setting an example: most every group knows those volunteers who show up at virtually every workday without fail, ready to chainsaw or get down to whatever the day's task is.

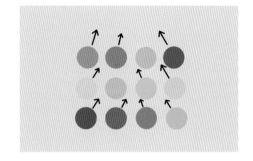

10 Core Qualities of a Steward

A handful of qualities (and probably a few more) can make for a successful steward.

1. Curiosity. Restoration contains many lifetimes of learning. You will never know all you need to.

2. Humility. Thinking you have it all figured out can be dangerous.

3. Ability to find and keep mentors. A panel of advisors is key. Nobody who does great restorations does them alone.

4. Willingness to lead. Even in the face of substantial ignorance, we go on the best available information.

5. Confidence to act. We know the riskiest move is to do nothing. "It's the 'we can do it' people who become leaders," says Stephen.

6. Eagerness to share with others, including sharing leadership.

7. At least a minimum of technical skills — functional botany, restoration techniques.

8. Proximity to the work. Helpful for making regular visits to one's site.

9. The ability to plan, act, assess, improve.

10. The ability to work well with people, especially those different from you.

Do I Know Enough to Be a Steward?

Even dedicated volunteers are sometimes hesitant to take on the mantle of steward. Underlying this feeling is often the sense that they don't know enough. "You're right," says Stephen. "At one level, you don't know enough. On the other hand, you know enough to help. And this area is just going to go downhill if you don't because there isn't anybody else."

"I sometimes quote ecologist Frank Egler, who said, 'Nature is more complicated than we think, and more complicated than we *can* think.' The human brain cannot *do it*. Now, we can get five people together — we can get an expert on plants, an expert on birds, an expert on soils, an expert on fire, whatever, and the hunter-gatherer group can increasingly approach knowing enough, but is going to be *waaay* short, at the very best.

"And so we're in the position of healers during hunter-gatherer times, or at various stages up until now, where medicine tries stuff, and you give somebody a certain drug, and maybe it works and maybe it doesn't. We're smart enough now that in many cases we say, 'Oh, here's the thing.' But in many cases, not. And if the patient's getting better, you keep doing that thing.

"And so, if an ecosystem is becoming more diverse and more filled with conservative species, that's one definition of a healthy patient. And you can often just determine that with a glance, but you can also determine it by a fairly rudimentary sampling process.

"And so, if you know enough to make that happen, then you know enough. And in many cases, people just say, 'Well, I can identify buckthorn and I can cut that,' and they can learn a little more in the process. And then they can do a little more and then learn a little more, and do a little more, and all along the way it's actually working. They knew enough to make the patient a little better. It's not terribly different from whether people know enough to be a parent."

Two Stewards, Two Styles

Stephen Packard's leadership style is organic, facilitative, even poetic. The late Tom Vanderpoel's was precise, factual, and practical. Both led some of the most effective and long-lived restoration efforts anywhere.

Stephen Packard

North Branch Restoration Project

- Tells inspiring stories in the lyrical language of nature and deep time, but also people and politics.

- Favors collective, facilitative approach, engaging others in ecological decisions, constantly asking "what do you think?"

- Deeply engaged in building regional culture through speaking, writing, blogs, and organizing.

- Operates by feel and intuition, on a case-by-case basis.

- Rarely gives answers — more often guides a questioner in thinking through a problem. A quizzer.

- Proactively hands over reins to give volunteers more first-hand experience and let them learn by doing. Gives relatively new volunteers opportunities to explain a concept or discovery to the rest of the group.

- A ready mentor.

- May begin tai chi in the middle of a meeting. (It's quite calming.)

Tom Vanderpoel

Citizens for Conservation

- Spoke in tactical, military terms: "Let's whack it!" "Hammer this thing!" "The 10 Warriors can go toe-to-toe with the invasives!"

- Made most ecological decisions and plans for CFC.

- Almost exclusively field-oriented and focused on CFC, partners' projects.

- Operated by applying logical, repeatable sequences based on experience and observation of results.

- Gave clear, precise answers to volunteers' questions.

- A math guy—could do arithmetic in his head and quickly calculate what it would take to do something well.

- "Never waste a volunteer's time" was a guiding principle. Had a Plan A, B, and C depending on conditions and who showed up.

- Remembered what volunteers cared about and what they were interested in and encouraged that.

- An avid sports fan—scheduled meetings around Blackhawks games.

Common Ground

The traits Stephen and Tom shared may be as responsible for their success as their differences:

- Endlessly curious and hungry to understand ecosystems
- Countless hours in the field, by themselves and in small groups
- Inexhaustible amounts of time for others
- Discussed frequently with peers (and played that role for each other)
- Committed to the end
- Jaw-dropping restoration results

Seeing Leaders

Lessons from the North Branch on identifying and cultivating future stewards and other group leaders.

1.   Look for Good Volunteers

Be ready to engage new people from the moment they arrive. Many lifelong volunteers and conservation professionals are hatched from that very first workday experience — if it's a positive one.

Potential leaders emerge almost immediately. "I asked Nachusa manager Bill Kleiman, 'How do you know if you have a good volunteer?' says Linda. "He said, 'If they show up.' And then if they show up four times. And then if they ask a question or they have an idea. You know, you begin to identify these people." Ask new volunteers what they want to do on the very first day.

2.   Listen for Offers of Ownership

Listen for people to express interests, and be ready to empower them. Have the list in your mind of the things your group needs, but prioritize someone taking ownership of something even if it's not on your list. Putting leadership-building above checking things off will more likely lead to a shared vision and a lasting group. In many ways, the secret technology on the North Branch is to say, 'They sound interested in this. I wonder if they'd take this on?'

3. Lavish the L-Word

Open your leadership circle with liberal application of the L-word. "Yeah, the word 'leader' — I love this word," says Eriko. "Because Stephen always uses it. I noticed this from the beginning. In the beginning, I thought, when I first was called a leader, that I was not a leader. But it makes you think like one — 'Oh, I can be kind of a small leader, a leader with a small l.'" Any invitation, subtle or explicit, goes a long way in encouraging would-be leaders. "I was coming often enough that when they were having a post-workday planning meeting, they invited me," says Eriko. "The group was open, not closed."

4. Encourage a Learning Culture

On the North Branch, volunteers build skills, judgment, and confidence gradually. There's a sort of unofficial progression: first-timer, regular volunteer, leader of a project or area, apprentice steward (working under the steward), and finally steward — sometimes "budding off" to lead at another site.

Learning opportunities are everywhere, from workdays and stewards' walks to more formal classes. Leaders at Somme Woods even created a "zone steward" system in which developing stewards take responsibility for a small section of preserve, under the tutelage of the site steward. "We try to create this atmosphere of accepting mistakes," says Linda, "where we're not critical of each other. We support each other; we encourage each other; we accompany each other to learn things. Some people know more than others...but you have these building blocks. And we all started knowing nothing."

Perfection isn't the ultimate goal, agrees Stephen. "It's worth a certain amount of sacrifice letting people do something not in the 100 percent best way, but maybe in the 65 percent best way. In some ways, the important thing wasn't so much that they in fact developed the way that was best. It's that they felt, 'This is ours. We're committed. I don't think Packard wants us to do it this way. We'll show him that it works.' I mean, they were committed to making this thing work. They just felt personally, 'This is us.' I think that's important."

Notes

About Stephen Packard

A pioneer in the volunteer-led restoration of native ecosystems since the 1970s, Stephen has helped thousands of "regular people" find their own connection with nature. His work with The Nature Conservancy of Illinois and Audubon – Chicago Region found him organizing efforts across the Chicago region, and he's shared that experience across the United States and abroad. He's been instrumental in efforts such as the Chicago Wilderness alliance, *Chicago Wilderness* magazine, Mighty Acorns, TNC's Volunteer Stewardship Network, the Wild Things Conference for People and Nature, Friends of the Forest Preserves, and the recently launched Friends of Illinois Nature Preserves, which seeks to build a more active consituency for the state's highest-quality remnant ecosystems. But Stephen's spiritual and ecological home base has long been the 90-acre Somme Prairie Grove in Northbrook, Illinois, where, as steward, he helped define the Midwestern oak savanna as an ecosystem distinct from prairie or woods. "Somme became more important to me than the other sites that I didn't have that relationship with, that didn't depend on me the way that one did," he says.

About Linda Masters

Since 1996, Linda has been the site steward of Somme Woods, just across Waukegan Road from Somme Prairie Grove. She has served as a professional ecologist and consultant with Conservation Design Forum and is currently a restoration specialist with Openlands. At the Morton Aboretum earlier in her career, she was a researcher on the original *Plants of the Chicago Region* – our local botanists' go-to "plant bible" – with Floyd Swink and Gerry Wilhelm. Linda and Stephen live together in Northbrook.

About Eriko Kojima

An apprentice steward, Eriko has volunteered with the North Branch since 2015. In her role as a zone steward at Somme Woods, she is responsible for the "Shooting Star" zone—20 acres of woods and wetlands. She's also a seed leader. Eriko's early career was in landscape architecture, and she has worked as a Japanese-English conference interpreter since 1990. She lives with her husband and daughter in Glenview.

TOOLSHED

The Scythe

WITH STEPHEN PACKARD

Want to look like the grim reaper? The scythe dates back at least to old Europe, where it was used to mow grass and harvest grains. In restoration, stewards use it for precision mowing of aggressive plants (especially where they're crowding out low-growers such as gentians) and sometimes to prepare areas for overseeding.

Deplete the reserves of invasive species such as tall goldenrod by cutting once or twice before flowering. Repeating this over multiple years will reduce plants.

Scything takes practice. Use the heft of the scythe to create a gentle, small cutting arc back and forth, like a pendulum. Find an easy rhythm — it shouldn't be a struggle.

The scythe can clear large swaths or be precise enough to clear around individual plants. A flick of the wrist can pick out single stems. Another handy use is to knock back tall vegetation along narrow footpaths.

Scythes can be ordered online. Opt for the lighter, more nimble grass scythe over a heavy brush scythe. European scythes tend to be more agile than the burlier American design. The best are made in Austria.

A range of blades can cut everything from grass to woody stems. The soft steel dulls fairly easily. Hone the blade frequently with a whetting stone.

Contributing Artists

Talent to match our ecosystems.

The painters, illustrators, and photographers listed here added a tremendous amount of life to this project. Their work celebrates the joy so many of us feel when we encounter truly wild places and wildlife. Many of these artists sell their art — please consider supporting them by hanging one of their wonderful works in your home or business.

Carrie Suzanne Carlson

With a background in scientific illustration for natural science and travel journals, teacher Carrie Carlson spends a lot of time with pen-and-ink and watercolor. She also loves linoleum block print. She and her family have been involved in restoration at Orland Grassland since that effort began.

carriecarlsonart.com
Instagram: bluebirdprintstudio
Etsy: CarrieCarlson

Philip Juras

Georgia native Philip Juras excels in representational oil paintings of intact natural landscapes. A little volunteering and lots of observing, especially in the Barrington area and Nachusa Grasslands, has greatly enriched his efforts to share a vision of the Illinois tallgrass prairie ecosystem.

philipjuras.com

Bobby Garro Sutton

Bobby Sutton works in pen, paint, even paper mache, and branched into digital media for this project. For pleasure, he's often drawn to the woods to sketch life. He has many happy recollections of sketching fringed gentians and prairie dock at Bunker Hill Forest Preserve in Chicago.

Linda W. Curtis

Botanist and sedge specialist Linda Curtis is a researcher, writer, and "carexmatic speaker" who also photographs the sedges she studies. The author of three books, she researches and writes for the Illinois Native Plant Society and Chiwaukee Prairie in Kenosha County.

curtistothethird.com

Kathleen Marie Garness

A scientific illustrator working traditionally in color and black-and-white as well as digitally, Kathy Garness is also a steward at Grainger Woods in Mettawa and Hosah Park in Zion. She most recently illustrated the updated glossary to *Flora of the Chicago Region*.

northamericanorchidcenter.org/featured-botanical-illustration

Jenny Vogt

Jenny Vogt typically works in soft pastels, using birds, the prairie, and wildlife as subjects. She finds artistic inspiration in the prairie each time she walks her bird monitoring routes at Poplar Creek and Spring Creek Forest Preserves in northwestern Cook County.

jennyvogt.com

Heeyoung Kim

Using watercolor, graphite pencil, and pen-and-ink to create traditional botanical art, Heeyoung discovered her craft while volunteering at Somme Prairie. Ryerson Woods has also become an inspiration for her artwork.

heeyoungkim.net

Don Parker

Favoring pen and colored pencil to illustrate nature, Don is a freelance writer, editor, and illustrator. He's been a restoration volunteer, organizer, and communicator for two decades, with the most hours logged at the Somme Preserves in Northbrook.

Image Credits

xi: Violet: Don Parker

xiii: Mink: Don Parker

1: Praire Reverie, linocut and watercolor. Carrie Suzanne Carlson / carriecarlsonart.com

3: Doug's Knob, Nachusa Grasslands. Philip Juras / philipjuras.com

5: Base plantings map: John Vanek / The Nature Conservancy

6–7: Bobby Garro Sutton

8–17: Don Parker

18–19: Inspired by Poplar Creek Prairie, oil on canvas. Philip Juras / philipjuras.com

21: Don Parker

23: Purple Prairie Clover, linocut and watercolor. Carrie Suzanne Carlson / carriecarlsonart.com

25–31: Don Parker

32–33: Bobby Garro Sutton

34–40: Don Parker

41: Spreadsheet: Rob Sulski

41: Photo: Don Parker

42–44: Don Parker

46: Courtesy Rob Sulski

47: Just Begin, ink, watercolor, white gel pen. Carrie Suzanne Carlson / carriecarlsonart.com

49: Don Parker

50–51: Bobby Garro Sutton

52: Linda W. Curtis / curtistothethird.com

54–55: Kathleen Marie Garness / kathleenmariegarness.com

56–57: Graphic: Don Parker

56–57: Photo: Donna Bolzman/Citizens for Conservation

58: Maps: Rob Neff and Jim Vanderpool / Citizens for Conservation

59–61: Don Parker

63: Don Parker

65: Oak Savanna, linocut and watercolor. Carrie Suzanne Carlson / carriecarlsonart.com

67: Courtesy Karen Glennemeier

68–69: Don Parker

70–71: Bobby Garro Sutton

72–73: Courtesy Karen Glennemeier

74–79: Don Parker

80: Courtesy Citizens for Conservation

81: Don Parker

81: Courtesy Friends of the Chicago River

82–87: Don Parker

88: Spreadsheet and Table: Don Parker

88: Map: Karen Glennemeier

89: Don Parker

90: Photo courtesy Karen Glennemeier

90: Rusty-patched Bumblebee & Coneflower, linocut and watercolor. Carrie Suzanne Carlson / carriecarlsonart.com

91: Dragonflies and Damselflies ink and watercolor. Carrie Suzanne Carlson / carriecarlsonart.com

93: Jenny Vogt

94–96: Don Parker

98–99: Bobby Garro Sutton

100–101: Birds and line graph: Don Parker

101: Bar graph: Karen Glennemeier

102–103: Don Parker (based on data and and maps courtesy Jenny Flexman)

104: Courtesy Jenny Flexman

105–113: Don Parker

114–115: Satellite image: Google, Landsat / Copernicus

114–115: Graphic overlay: Don Parker

116: Courtesy Jenny Flexman

116: *Quercus macrocarpa*, linocut and watercolor. Carrie Suzanne Carlson / carriecarlsonart.com

117: Henslow's Sparrows, ink and watercolor. Carrie Suzanne Carlson / carriecarlsonart.com

118: Bobby Garro Sutton

120: Detail: Bobby Garro Sutton

121: Don Parker

122–123: Bobby Garro Sutton

124–125: Heeyoung Kim / heeyoungkim.net

127: Courtesy Stephen Packard

128–131: Don Parker

132: Heeyoung Kim / heeyoungkim.net

133: Don Parker

134–137: Bobby Garro Sutton

138 (top): Courtesy Stephen Packard

138 (middle): Courtesy Linda Masters

138: (bottom) Courtesy Eriko Kojima

139: Don Parker

140: Sandhill Cranes in Flight, linocut reduction print. Carrie Suzanne Carlson / carriecarlsonart.com